Love, *Peace* & Gravity:

The Journey of a Lifetime

DOMONIQUE HARVEY

USA

ISBN: 978-0-578-94121-9

Listening to the clouds, feeling the wind, looking for a sign,
tasting your presence…

Table of Contents

Introduction 5

Section One 7

Chapter 1: Soul Mates 9

Chapter 2: Our Third Floor Attic 37

Chapter 3: Tough Pill To Swallow 57

Chapter 4: Nightmare Of A Dreamer 67

Chapter 5: Reassuring 81

Section Two 89

Chapter 6: Back On Track 91

Chapter 7: The Relapse 101

Chapter 8: Journey To Wellness 119

Chapter 9: The Final Chapter 137

Peace & Gravity 159

Acknowledgments 163

About The Author 171

INTRODUCTION

Ever wondered how the universe works? Ever thought to yourself, that there was a secret language both spoken and understood? Or how it all can work in your favor? What about the number of wonders of the world there actually are? The one question that I've always pondered in the back of my mind since I was a teenager: *how do we prepare for death*? I asked myself this question on many occasions. Life eventually gave me the answers that I've been searching for. I've lost a lot of loved ones along this journey which helped me to understand that death makes our lives important and meaningful--it creates priority, and gives us perspective to focus on what and who is urgent to us. While on this search, I found that Love works the same way. Love is also the language of the universe. Learning life lessons prepares you for life and death--think about it. It's a similar phenomenon as the birth of a child; "the nest" should be prepared--so to speak. All things have to be in order. Similar to death, things must be arranged and prepared, but when the smoke clears, love stands amongst the smoldering flames. The love you have for your child is ever-present before birth. Long before you met this tiny human or touched their little fingers and toes, your heart overflowed with love for this being. In this same regard, you love the person that has passed on and if you're lucky enough to get an opportunity, make sure you know they love you. I believe that and I found this out for myself the hard way.

SECTION ONE

CHAPTER 1
SOUL MATES

My fiance Aaron and I had been together for 3 years. Madly in love with one another, we always believed that we were deeply connected; we had a cosmic connection. We read each other's energy no matter where we are, because we had done so in a past life. Aaron and I have been very special together and we have impacted each other in a past life, the present, and in the next lifetime. We believe this wholeheartedly because love, trust, communication and understanding between us came so easily. Aaron and I have been through such turbulence in our relationship.

The beauty of being in love with your soulmate is that you always have someone who caters to your each and every need. Whether it's emotionally, physically or spiritually; the list is endless. That person is there and knowing that love is reciprocated makes a continual cycle of blissful happiness. Experiencing love without conditions or contingencies doesn't happen everyday but for us it did. We never really had to say much and wanted to tell each other everything. Aaron was everything that I wanted and needed in a man plus more. He would tell me how much he loved me all the time and I would do the same. With us, it was always the "why" of it all. You can tell every person on the street that you love them, but it's in the action; love is a verb.

I met my soulmate years ago in the seventh grade. At that time we were too young to know what true love was. But we always shared good feelings after we saw each other. Just in brief interactions, we felt so drawn to one another. Aaron Harvey was not your average guy. He is always respectful and nice to everyone he meets. He is intelligent, sweet, funny, charming, talented, brilliant, well dressed, charismatic; a certified genius or an anomaly, if you will. If you saw me in middle school, and judged a book by its cover, you definitely would not think that we would be a match. I did not dress feminine; I mostly dressed like a boy and wore my hair in a messy, puffy ponytail. He always had this sense of calmness about him that I was so attracted to. Aaron has always been such a huge dreamer. He would always come up with the most far-fetched ideas, but would find ways on how they would work. Unfortunately, I did not have the privilege of learning this until much later. Aaron and I never really said much to each other during our middle school years, but he could take my breath away with just one look.

Sadly, that was the same year I had to move, and with moving I had to switch schools. During that time, Aaron had just returned to New Jersey from Maryland--right about the same time I ended up moving. According to the school's regulations, even though I literally moved two blocks from my old house, I was no longer a resident of that school district. Luckily Aaron and I were only one grade apart and ended up going to the same high school. Aaron was in high school one year ahead of me. Transitioning into high school opened my eyes to realize that he had become *"Mr. Popular"* or *"The mayor of the school"*, as his mother called him. There was no way I thought *"Mr. Popular"* would have any interest in me. I still dressed like a boy and styled my hair in the same weird, puffy and messy ponytail. I wasn't what our generation considered to be average either. I was quiet, yet smart, talented, driven, funny, very tomboyish and just different from the rest of the girls in my grade. I was an introvert who stayed to myself a lot during those years. Everyone knew me though. They often referred to me as "the girl that sings." He assured me that those were the very things that he was attracted to and made him fall for me.

In high school, Aaron finally worked up the courage to ask me to be a part of his musical project that he had been working on. Aaron often found his voice and expression through music. By this time, he was a very talented rapper and was well-known in our town for his clever freestyling abilities. He had a way with words like a poet. His style of storytelling makes a person feel as if they were right there with him when it happened. I too expressed myself through song. I was so shy, yet excited and nervous at the same time I agreed to sing. We exchanged numbers and the very next day we were discussing how he wanted this song to be done. By the time the weekend rolled around we were on our way to the recording studio. That's when I found out he had a girlfriend. My little heart was crushed, so I packed up my ego as we recorded the song and went our separate ways yet again. It was not until years later Aaron told me that he and his 'girlfriend' were not exclusively dating. She kind of just followed him around. I only wished I had known that information sooner. Since we're from the same town we always found ourselves stealing a moment to interact if even for a few minutes. Years would pass before we would see each other again, but we would periodically end up at the same places at the same time.

In our pre-teenage years, we were in middle school, and as teenagers we were in high school. It was not until we were in our twenties when he decided to show up again. We both worked at Meadowlands Stadium for a day.

I was 23 years old and had joined my first ever bikini contest because I was in pursuit of a modeling career and he was there at the very same contest. He wasn't there to show off his body in a bikini, but to end the show with his rhymes. A few weeks prior I was approached by someone at a car show. He asked if I would like to be in a bikini contest and I would be given $50 whether I win or lose. So I figured why not, what do I have to lose? Hard to believe but I actually didn't make it past the first round. Aside from Aaron being the smartest in class and in life, his love for music outshined any other form of creativity. It was as if everything he touched turned to gold. But, what are the odds--we hadn't seen each other in years, yet here we are in a corner of this huge stadium. Amongst thousands of people, we manage to find each other again! When we got a free moment, we talked behind the tent. He had asked if I still sang. I responded, "of course, music is always something that keeps finding me." He then responded, "let me hear something." Here I go again, totally nervous and shy, yet feeling a sense of comfort at the same time. I began to bellow out lyrics to a Jasmine Sullivan song titled, "Lions, Tigers and Bears." He was completely in awe of my voice and said *"damn girl, you still got it!"* We started walking around and it started to feel as if we were on a date. We got lost in conversation and into each other so calmly and so easily that we really forgot that we were on the clock set to work.

While I waited around for the contest to start I was approached by a man who represented Cooper Tires, one of the largest rubber and tire companies in America. This man asked if I was a model. I responded *"why yes I am"*. He then proceeded to hand me a camera and asked if I would stand next to random pedestrians as they walked by the Cooper tire tent for advertisement purposes. I was originally paired with another model. But she had stepped away for some reason. To my surprise there was Aaron stepping in to help. As we walked around the crowded stadium, Aaron stopped nearly everyone that walked past and convinced them to take a picture with me. I was so impressed at his persistence and approach. After a while his phone rang and I assumed it was business. Previously working with him in the studio, I already knew that he had taken his time and music very seriously. He allowed nothing to get in the way of that, and not even a platonic date with me--the woman he didn't know he was in love with. So after he was done with his call, he looked at me, giggled and said, "I was enjoying my time with you so much that I forgot I had work to do, but I'll be cheering for you later." I blushed so hard that my cheeks began to hurt. Finally the stage was set and the contestants were being prepped for the contest. Looking out into the crowd, I couldn't find him at first but then I heard my name being yelled from the back of the crowd. Aaron stands at 5 feet and 5 inches tall, so although I couldn't see him, I heard him loud and clear. He definitely kept his promise, as I walked onto that stage I could hear his voice above everyone else, all the way in the back screaming so loudly for me. He made me feel so prized and special that day.

We had some of the most memorable moments in high school, but fast forward past those years, we live very different lives than we remembered. Aaron wasn't hanging around the school hallways shooting the breeze with his friends, and I wasn't walking around the school hallways singing my little ol' heart out for the fellow students. He is now a single father and I am engaged to be married. My 23rd birthday had passed not too long before Aaron and I ran into each other. I had recently gotten engaged to a school teacher and was living in Roselle Park, New Jersey now. I was living a cushy life, driving fast and fancy cars and enjoying life. Even with that in mind, for some strange reason it was still so hard walking away from him that day. It was as if the universe was trying to tell us something. We were just so stuck on the fact that we always felt lighter after our interactions. Timing just could not have been worse. Although we always knew there was something magical between us, we knew that we could never act on it. It felt almost as if God played a cruel joke on us. Like God is saying: *here's your soulmate but you can't have him.* Maybe we just simply weren't ready, so I made peace with it and carried on with life.

Three years later after our platonic date at the stadium, I lived a completely different life. I was married in my late twenties with a baby girl living comfortably as a housewife. One day, I logged onto social media as usual, scrolled for a while and looked into my inbox. Then I proceeded to go to the home page and hit the refresh button, only to find that Aaron had posted photos. To my surprise they were wedding photos--his wedding photos. There I was sitting there trying to muster up a smile as I watched the man of my dreams dance with another woman. Talk about shattered dreams, my heart was in a million pieces. *"Why?"* I asked myself. *"Why didn't I steal him when I had the chance"*? Then shortly after I asked myself, *"how can I even be upset about him marrying someone else. When I myself had already built a life with someone else too?* A week had gone past and I couldn't log onto Facebook. Afraid that he'd post more photos and videos that I had no interest in seeing. Finally, I convinced myself that it was silly for me to feel this way. So I logged into Facebook and before my brain could catch up to my fingertips, I opened my messages. I scrolled to the search bar and typed "Aaron Harvey". His profile page popped up. At that point I gulped and began to think to myself *"I just gotta know if he's really happy."* I proceeded to type the words "Hey! How are you?" He responded, "Hey! I'm good but I know you didn't reach out just to say hi." In my mind, this minor interaction between us was equivalent to the feeling you get during your teenage years when you call your crush and they say hello, and then you hang up out of sheer nervousness. I had nothing to say; I was stuck, and no action was taken. My initial reason when I reached out was to get an idea of where he was in life. Was he really happy with the woman he recently married? But, I didn't know what to say. So rather than make a fool of myself I didn't say a word after that. I was too chicken and afraid to say what I really wanted to say. I wanted to scream through the screen and say, *"Hey, let's get divorced and run away together,"* but I was too afraid to say something like that so that never happened. We were well into our twenties and were both parents. He was a father of two beautiful little girls, Grace and Cambria and now someone's husband. I chalked it up as Aaron being *"the one that got away"* Or as he would often call me *"the great white buffalo"*. We let some more years pass us by.

Life as we knew it took us in some weird and uncomfortable twists and turns. The universe conspired yet again through social media. I wasn't very active on Instagram or Facebook at this time, but a good friend of mine convinced me to use it for networking purposes. I already had an account, but I never used it. So I had a lot of old classmates and friends on my following list and didn't even know it. Lo and behold, Aaron was one of the first people that requested me as a friend. As soon as I logged in, his profile photo was right there on my phone screen. Just as devilishly handsome as

I remembered. I paused for a second and allowed my heart to skip a beat. Then I began to do a little digging and researching, and what do you know, no wedding photos. No pictures of him with any women, just him and his creative visual art that he created for his music! Right then and there I made the decision to reach out and this time I started by giving him a compliment on his creativeness. I told him that I was glad that he was still doing music. We talked off and on through social media for a few minutes a day. Then minutes turned to hours. At last he gave me his number, and said he wanted to talk to me when I had time. Feelings of nervousness, excitement and confidence struck me at once, and I was so happy that I had taken the first step. I knew that this time around I wasn't letting him get away. The day came for us to hear each other's voice over the phone. He sounded just the same; always proper and well-spoken. To my surprise he wanted me to take part in another project. This time I would be his leading lady in an upcoming music video he was planning to produce. I happily accepted the position. After talking on the phone for hours the conversation went from business to personal. We asked the questions that we always wanted to know from the beginning of our conversation. Woefully, I was still unhappily married and near separation at this point. Aaron revealed to me that he was recently separated from his wife. Both of us felt the connection right away as we always did when stepping into each other's vicinity. We knew within seconds of hearing each other's voice that if we got together we would be inseparable.

As time went on Aaron and I talked every single day all day. He gave me something to look forward to every morning. Anytime he sent a text message I got goosebumps. Just the anticipation of what was to come was so exciting. I was literally floating on air each day. It felt amazing to know that I was this man's first thought in the morning and his last thought in the evening. Meanwhile, in my household at the time it was the complete opposite. I found myself in a Catch 22 situation. On one hand, I had finally caught the eye and attention of this wonderful man who I knew would be a perfect match for me, but he was still in a touchy situation with his wife. On the other hand, I was living with the man that I already committed to, but was nowhere near a perfect match for me. Aaron and I completely ignored the reality of the situation at hand and decided to choose happiness. Never with the intention of hurting anyone, we just had enough of settling. We continued to have frequent phone conversations. We texted a lot, I mean messages by the hundreds per day.

One day I decided that I wanted to see him. He asked to spend time with me a few times before, but it wasn't always easy getting away and finding the time. We made plans a few times but they fell through. I would have to rearrange some plans because of my daughter or something that day just wouldn't allow it. And there was the fact that I was trying to play hard-to- get at one point. So I would tell him I had plans on certain days or I had to go into work. I grew tired of the housewife role and had two jobs. But In all actuality, I was kind of scared. The connection over the phone is so endearing that I was actually afraid of what would happen if we were face-to-face. *Will I be able to contain myself around him? Am I going to pounce like a dog in heat? Or would I just play it cool?* All these questions played out in my head.

Finally, the day came where I was brave enough to find out how much better life could be with this wonderful person. I remember driving to his house with the feeling of butterflies in my stomach as I turned each corner and stopped at each intersection. It wasn't a long drive from my house to Aaron's, but it seemed like it had taken me forever to get there that evening. I finally turned onto his street and called him to let him know that I had arrived. Before he came to get me from my car I was so giddy and anxious. I kept checking myself out in every mirror, and then came the moment of truth. As he approached my car I took a deep breath, exhaled then exited the car. Having never felt this way before I didn't know how to act. We actually met in the middle of the street and hugged each other. It seemed as if every object and being stood still! There were no cars passing, or people walking on the sidewalk, no voices were heard, and it was as if the trees disappeared. Time stood still for a moment and nothing or nobody else existed around us. Moments like this are only read about in cheesy romance novels, or love scenes from romantic comedy movies. It just amazed me that he had put all of my broken pieces back together with just one hug. After that we walked up to his attic apartment and talked while listening to his music. It was comforting to see that he was just as nervous as I was, if not more. The word "nervous" is not in Mr. Harvey's vocabulary. Once we moved past all the jitters, we just stared into each other's eyes in amazement. We literally gazed into each other's eyes most of the night. Then he breaks the silence, grabs my hand and says, "I really can't believe you're here with me." I smiled and blushed the rest of the night. My soul was at peace, my spirit was calm, and my mind rested in pure silence as I was taking the entire experience in. The most magical part about this night was that there was no physical contact, other than holding hands. We enjoyed each other's company.

After that evening, Mr. Harvey had become my addiction and I was hooked on him. We stole every moment together that we could manage. Whether we were enjoying a bite to eat, walking in the park, or meeting at a friend's house, Aaron and I were just so elated to be in the presence of the person we had always known as "the one". Our conversations were always filled with depth. By depth, I mean profound. Aaron is very articulate and loves life. His knowledge about a variety of topics has always been so attractive to me. I love to listen to him speak about topics ranging from aliens to jews, gems and crystals. I looked forward to spending every waking moment with this incredible being. I absolutely fell in love with the way he is always so attentive and affectionate--something I was longing for in a relationship that was being starved of by my husband. Aaron knew things about me in the first few days that my husband never paid attention to, or picked up on in the 13 years we were together. He always expresses how he loves the way I smile and how he wishes I show my teeth more. Aaron noticed how self-conscious I was about my crooked tooth. He said that it was one of my best features and convinced me not to hide it. His mind was so intricate that he moved at times as if he had an orchestra playing in his mind. The way he sits with his right ankle resting on his left knee, and his right elbow digging into his right thigh as his chin rests between his thumb and pointer fingers of his right hand. It was like he was so sure of himself; very secure at all times. Aaron is always certain about practically everything--the woman on his arm (me), the watch he wears and the way he designs each moment. What more could a woman ask for in a man?

Finding myself completely head over heels for him in a matter of days was quite the shocker. I grew up around a lot of male figures in my family, and with time I adopted some of their bad relationship habits. So I ran away from love a few times, but this time I was running towards it full speed ahead. No matter what the outcome would be, I was willing to take a chance to get to know this man. As we approached the third week of continuous non-stop communication, I realized that this is where I needed and wanted to be, especially after the relationship had become sexual. Aaron made my body do things that I didn't even know I enjoyed, but most importantly, he let me know that he wanted so much more than just sex. I already knew this because I never experienced passion on the level I had with anyone before him. The ecstasy and passion I experienced being intimate with Aaron was so beautiful that I actually cried and he kissed my tears. I found myself gazing directly into his eyes with each stroke. I never wanted to forget that feeling of newness. Normally after experiencing sex in a relationship, it tends to get old fast. I savored each second as he penetrated my soul. For a short guy he was well endowed. I soon found out where his extra inches of height had gone. It seemed as if he had keys to my frontal lobe that no man before him had possessed. My body trembled as he kissed me so softly and stared directly into my eyes and gently stroked and stroked. I felt every inch enter my body and sent me to another universe as I stopped breathing for a second. As we looked at each other in the moment of ecstasy his eyes too began to well up with tears. This is what I had imagined my very first time should've felt like. But, he made me feel like this was my first time being intimate with anyone. I felt like a virgin all over again, not just in the physical sense, but mentally I felt like this was a brand new experience for both of us as we explored each other's bodies. We had fantasized about this moment, but never imagined it would be like this.

I wanted to follow him wherever he would go. Some days he would text me because I couldn't talk on the phone with him because my husband was around. So we texted back and forth throughout the course of the day. By night time, we were text messaging "good night" to one another and it began to escalate to "good night my love", to eventually, "I love..." I caught myself mid-way between the message where I was about to tell him that I loved him. I was pretty sure he felt the same way because he showed me constantly. I still wasn't sure if he was ready to hear those words from my mouth. I deleted the text to the message almost immediately, but I felt that he should know that I almost texted him. Jokingly but seriously I replied, "I'm not gonna tell you what I almost said to you just now." Aaron's response was what I already expected. His text reply read, "Babe, you don't even have to say it because I already know." It was like he could practically read my soul through text! It was nothing short of amazing how I never had to tell him much, and he would already just know--almost as if he had telepathic psychic abilities. We ended the conversation so beautifully that evening. His last text to me that night was a question. He began by asking if I believed that I would actually leave my husband and be with him. This is how that conversation went:

My response was, "Yes. Regardless, I'm leaving. I'm no longer happy here and I'm already with you." I always made it clear to him that I was leaving my marriage for myself, and not for him. He understood and admired my honesty. He went on to reply, "I love the way you look at me, the way you see my vision and understand my crazy thoughts. I just need your help, love." I asked, "with what?" He said, "Just be my Gravity. Remain forever constant. My love is deep and unconditional. I'll always be true, and you'll know it because we connect that way." I took a deep breath after reading that, and got choked up. I responded, "babe, you have ALL of me and we have forever and a day ahead of us. I'm not going anywhere." We didn't give each other lil pet names that most couples use like 'boo', 'honey pie', or 'pookie bear.' He gave me the name "*Gravity*" because I held him down. I called him "*Peace*" because that's how I felt being around him. He calmed my spirit peacefully. I knew that Aaron had been through some rough and toxic relationships prior to me. I know he wanted and longed for the exact same things that I searched for in a mate. Reassurance and stability of true intimacy; unbreakable bond and loyalty. We both wanted unconditional love without contingencies. We found it in each other that love, energy, and admiration carried us through the void that we had been missing. He always believed from the very beginning of our relationship that we would be the couple that everyone would look at to see what true happiness looked like. He couldn't have been more right.

Aaron and I officially started dating in July 2018. The perfect time to fall in love. The birds were chirping and we were the two happiest people on the planet. Still living with my daughter and her father at the time, and trying to find a way out of the marriage was very challenging. But in Aaron-like fashion, he found a loophole. He had asked me if I would do him a favor. Without hesitation I said "of course!" He asked if I would travel with him. I asked him where to go first. Aaron had asked if I would travel to Italy with him. He meant in our dreams, and I let him know that I would go to the end of the world with him. He began telling me about a little restaurant there that had the most beautiful love story behind it. It's called Osteria Francescana, in Modena, Italy. So elated and honored that this man had made big plans even if it was in our dreams made me feel like the luckiest woman in the world. The fact that he even shared that story with me let me know that he truly felt that I was "the one" for him. His great white buffalo had returned to him, and he was now living out a childhood dream. Aaron wanted to stay connected to me in those moments that we couldn't spend together, so he would ask me to meet him somewhere different in our dreams every time we were apart.

Our second place was Paris, on a specific boardwalk and as crazy as it may sound we would really meet in our dreams. Our souls were so attached that I would see him while I slept. We connected through astral travel, which would be exactly where we agreed to meet. When we made time to meet in real life we would discuss how realistic our dreams would be. It was such a wonderful feeling to see his energy around even if he wasn't physically in my presence. By the time our one month anniversary came around, he had something special planned for us. I arrived at his house at around 7:30pm. We both hopped into his car, kissing and hugging, then he turned to me with a huge smile on his face and kept kissing me again and again. He could always get me to show full teeth and gums while I'm smiling. I began to wonder why we haven't driven off yet. He finally looks at me, digs into his pocket and pulls out a set of gold keys. Completely oblivious to what was happening, I was speechless. He said, "babe, with your current situation being what it is, you're gonna' need a place to go to get away. These are the keys to my place and you have complete access even if I'm not home. If you need a place to escape to just cry, because there will be tears, just know that you can come here." My jaw hit the floor of his car. I had no idea that was coming. All I could exclaim was "thank you baby," while blushing and my eyes welled up with tears. I was so touched by this gesture. Not only did it mean that I had complete access to him, but it proved that I was the only woman that he wanted. Before we pulled off and right after Aaron gave me my own set of keys to his apartment, he laughed and let out a sigh of relief. He giggled and said "I was so nervous, I had these keys made weeks ago. I just couldn't find the right time or right way to give them to you. "I replied, "that was perfect but anyway and any time you did it would have never mattered." We finally drove away from his house and hit the highway. The anticipation was getting the best of me. He would not give me a clue as to where we were headed. We eventually ended up at the Hoboken Pier and oh what a sight it was to see. I left my phone in the car purposely because I didn't want to miss not one moment of it. I looked forward to taking in all of the sights. There were vibrant electrifying lights and water with tall buildings reaching across the waterfront. There were party cruise boats passing by, and the atmosphere was so beautiful. There was no way I wanted to experience it through a lens. Now most people probably wouldn't be impressed by water and lights, but it never required much to put a smile on my face, especially coming from Aaron. We were both hopeless romantics and having the one you call your soulmate to share these moments with made it a million times better. The simplest things in life will make a person happy and overjoyed. Being with someone you connect with so naturally is absolutely the most fulfilling feeling in the world. Aaron and I felt like we were best friends our whole lives. The level of comfort was so automatic and effortless--that's what a soulmate is. It's not someone you have a few things in common with but someone who feels like home and Aaron Harvey felt like a peaceful refuge. A little time went past and we were frequently seeing more and more of each other. There were times I would pretend to leave for work very early in the morning, and call out but would use my golden keys very often. I was living a double life until Aaron told me how much he hated when I had to leave. He looked at me with irresistibly adorable puppy dog eyes, and said, "babe you know you don't have to leave--you can just stay."

I smirked and laid back down. Aaron knew he had me right where he wanted me. We made love for a third time before falling asleep.

I knew I had responsibilities to tend to but I also knew that my husband did not want to let go either. So this was Aaron's subtle way of allowing me to let go of my husband and slowly move in with him. He got his wish one night when I ended up spending the night and unintentionally overslept. I did not return home until 6:30am the next morning. Only to be greeted by an angry husband. All I could think of in the back of my mind was, *"welp I wanted out of this marriage so here I go."* Facing the issue head on, he had already suspected that I was cheating, because I would be on my phone constantly. It was always stuck to my hand like glue. I told my husband of 6 years for the umpteenth time that I was done and wanted a divorce. He yelled at the top of his lungs with anger in his eyes as he told me to leave and to go back to where I came from. I grabbed my daughter, and he tried to grab her back from me as I attempted to exit the apartment. I darted for the door again with my daughter in tow as she was crying hysterically. This time I successfully made it outside. When I reached my car I called Aaron right away and told him what happened. He said okay and that he already made space for my daughter Sky.

Aaron and Sky had met a few times before so she knew him and was comfortable. Although I had the freedom that I always wanted, I regret putting my child in the center of the affair. I never wanted her to witness her parents arguing. As I drove to a nearby park to meet with Aaron I realized that I had done it. I finally got the nerve to leave the unhappy marriage that I had been trying to escape for years but never had the courage or nerve to leave. I had just freed myself from being what is known as a "kept woman". I was no longer just a trophy wife. Even though my daughter didn't understand it at the time, I had removed her from a toxic environment. I drove in the direction towards my way to happiness that day.

Our first night actually living together was incredible. Aaron and I talked all night after my daughter fell asleep. We discussed what had taken place earlier and he was concerned about how I felt about it. Completely in shock that I had finally done it, I told him, "I am ok I feel so free. I wish it had happened a little differently, like I wish we could've had a civil and mature conversation, but I also knew the situation was beyond repair and communication." But the only thing I could think about was how considerate Aaron was about it all. He always knew what to do and say at the appropriate time. He knew where it hurt and I didn't have to say a word. His hugs and kisses were all that was needed at that moment. All it required was a simple smile and everything was fine. The work of my soulmate walked me through a tough time in my life. Aaron did exactly what he was designed to do. I had been rewarded with the perfect man who could love me in the manner and respect I needed to be cared for. Finally, I found my peace.

"Gravity looks deeper into the windows of my soul, then you'll know. You'll see a reflection of yourself whole and complete."

AARON HARVEY

CHAPTER 2
OUR THIRD FLOOR ATTIC

Most women as little girls fantasize about living a fairytale dream. We want the perfect wedding, the big house, the prince charming, the white picket fence, and the fancy car. But when reality sets in as you get older you begin to realize that none of that is real. Life doesn't happen the way we plan it to happen. Maybe if you're lucky you'll get 2 out of 5 of those things. For me, I got my prince charming, no fancy car, but I drove a decent car. I had a nice wedding. I just wasn't married to my charming prince and there was no white picket fence or huge multi-room home. Instead, Aaron and I had a third floor attic apartment. Just to clarify, an attic is not technically considered an actual apartment, but we made it home! It wasn't much to look at; the hallway had a leaky ceiling, and there was a smell of mildew when you first walked in. The floor was also missing tiles. Then as a visitor finally reached the third floor, the steps were irregular and gave you quite the workout. As soon as a visitor walks in they're standing in the kitchen. The floors were uneven, and you could literally feel where the floor dipped into a hill when you walked. There was no molding around the doorways or floors. So I stuffed paper towels in the cracks so we could have privacy while using the bathroom. Our bedroom was the coldest and draftiest during winter months and the hottest in the summer. Just imagine, heat rises so we would actually be cooking up there. At one point we didn't have air conditioning. Not only could we not afford one, but our window in the bedroom was not standard size. The window was so small that the air conditioner wouldn't even fit anyway. If you looked below the window there was a hole there where you could see directly outside. It wasn't huge but it was enough to where one could see through it as a peephole. In the girl's room there was a gap where the wall and floor met. You could actually see the fiberglass insulation sticking out. But there was a little piece of wood that we covered it up with and it reminded us of the little mouse door from the movie "Coraline."

Our daughters Grace, Cammie and Sky (the girls) loved it though. They didn't live with us full time, but when they were here every other weekend they used their imagination to overlook the flaws. Speaking of mice, we had so many during one point that we should've been charging them rent. We started out with practically nothing. Even though Aaron was living there for a short period of time before I moved in, he wasn't working at the time. With him just leaving an unhappy marriage, all he had was one suitcase full of his things, a mattress on the floor, a fold up table and chair and a refrigerator. Imagine that, a month prior I was just driving a Mercedes Benz, living in a nice fully furnished apartment situated in a quiet town. Fast forward a short time later, and now I'm living in a mouse infested attic with my prince charming. On top of all that, we had the noisiest neighbors in the middle of the neighborhood. With that being said, we were still the two happiest people in the world. None of that mattered because we had each other. We looked at our relationship as a do-over. We had a chance to start over and the setting or location didn't matter. We made that house a home. We named our humble abode *"Harvey'z World"*. It was like our own little planet. As we sat in our bedroom one day we talked about how we lived in so many different places over time, but it had taken us to come back to our home town where we both grew up. With nothing but a dollar and a dream to start over, together.

Our relationship blossomed rapidly. Our days seemed like months, and even though we had only lived together a month, it seemed like we already lived an eternity together. Time didn't exist on our planet. Our apartment wasn't much to look at but somehow we found beauty in it. We had the crappiest view in the back of the house. If you looked at it for the first time, it was really just a row of houses across the backyard. From left to right there was just a view of buildings, balconies and fire escapes. However, depending on what view you wanted you'd have to time it just right. For instance, if you sat by that window at 5am, you could hear a pin drop and know that there is a family of tiny little birds in the tree that sat in the middle of our backyard. They only came out at a certain time of day. You could hear the birds communicating from tree to tree. Occasionally, the neighbor to the left of us would come out on the fire escape at around 11am to steal a moment to himself. It was almost as if he was hiding the fact that he smoked from his wife. Then at night you can watch the airplanes fly by. Sometimes they sounded so close that you would think that they were going to land on our roof. Aaron loved sitting by that window during that time of night. I remember hugging him around his neck as he sat by that kitchen window one night. Sitting in our half computer chair that was covered in paint--the chair looked like we found it in someone's garbage. He just gazed at the sky. He turned and gave me a kiss and said "they come every 13 minutes." With his phone in his hand pointing at the airplanes, he timed them. So, I sat with him quietly and waited for the next one to come. He pointed at his phone as we heard the plane coming and looked up at me and said "told ya". I looked at his phone and sure enough, it read 13 minutes and 20 seconds. We smiled at each other lovingly; his face just said it all. He looked at me and I could tell that he was just appreciative and elated at my mere presence. Just the fact that I sat there with him just to time the airplanes was all he wanted. I looked at him and all I could think was I'm so amazed at the fact that we both found so much happiness in something as simple as watching airplanes. We realized that we genuinely enjoy each other's company and energy, and that we truly value and appreciate, breathe and live for these very moments. Noticing that we really longed for whatever it was that we found in each other, I only wondered what else was trapped in that beautiful mind of his. Sitting by that window was a stress reliever . If we would argue, which was hardly ever, that was where we could find the other one.

We sat there to clear our overthinking and cluttered minds. We found joy in our mouse infested, unlevel floors, drafty walls and irregular steps of a place we called home. We made miracles in the kitchen; all of our cooking appliances plugged into the wall in order to be used. Being that the apartment was technically considered illegal there was no way we could have a stove up there. But we both were no strangers to struggle, so we made do with what we had. I grew up in a single parent home. My father was a truck driver when I was a little girl so he was gone a lot of the time. He would drop in for a full-time visit about twice a week. My mother struggled with rent and bills and of course dad helped. Dad also had a lot more children and households to visit. I'm not sure how many other children my father had at that time. I know that if I counted now he was at seventeen children before he passed away in 2016. I remember I had to light candles because there was no money to pay the electric bill or maybe my mother simply forgot. With six children running around she may have forgotten a time or two, but we never let that stop us from having fun. We just made it an adventure. We'd tell scary stories until we got sleepy. Aaron also grew up in similar conditions. With his mom as a single parent and on the go often and his father being mainly absent made him a latch key kid by the age of nine. Aaron didn't have much either. He also didn't have any siblings to share scary stories with at the time, however he did have a few friends. He once told me a story about how he almost cried at a friend's house. He said that his friend would often ask if Aaron could stay for dinner. I guess that particular night his friend's mom didn't want extra company and remarked "no, doesn't he have a house?" Faced with the sad truth that yes he had a home but he'd almost always be there alone with no food on the table because his mother worked a lot. Aaron and his mother lived out of state with no other family close by. Aaron learned how to hold his own and made an adventure of it also. He read a ton of books to occupy his time. So to say the least we appreciated the little bit that we had and never had taken anything for granted--not even each other's company. When we first started dating, he took me on my very first ferry ride on the New York waterway. We walked to the side of this huge ferry and pointed at fish, the Statue of Liberty, and the islands that surrounded us on the way over. Aaron looked at me and said " if you think about it, it's kind of ominous, our relationship. It's how it happens in some movies. We finally find the one we were meant to be with and then tragedy comes. Someone dies and the other is left here alone." I was never too keen on the morbid conversations. So I told him "well, nobody is dying today so let's enjoy it!"

Starting from humble beginnings helped us appreciate the fact that we had a chance to make this raggedy house a home-- our home. We slowly began to put things in order. Aaron went back to work, which now made it so we could afford a little more than just rent and food. Date nights we could eat more than the $1 slices of pizza in the city. Although, those slices were very good! According to him it's because of the water in New York City that made the pizza so much better. We absolutely loved date nights in the city! Even when we only had enough for the train ride, a couple slices, and one soda. Aaron loved NY so much that most of his jobs as a broker were in the Big Apple. He began taking odd jobs in warehouses here and there when I first moved in. While I worked for an import company in Port Newark, New Jersey. But, that did not last long at all. He was way too smart, ambitious and charismatic to waste his time and talent doing warehouse work. So he applied to a number of offices anywhere from Jersey City to New York City. When I tell you he was different this is what I mean. While setting up all of his interviews he was also planning to take me on a surprise date. He saw how hard I was working, between actual hard work while taking care of our children. He noticed that I was exhausted and figured I could use a break. He asked me to take the day off, and so I did. He killed two birds with one stone that day. We actually had a date while he went on a series of interviews. There we were on an adventure together. Creating so many beautiful memories. We caught train after train walked block after block. I saw the inside of some of the most beautiful buildings that I thought I would ever see. Aaron opened my eyes up to a whole new world that I never knew existed. We ended the date by having lunch in the city and of course he got offered a position from every single place he had an interview. One of the companies didn't even let us make it to the corner before they called and asked if he could start on Monday! I was so proud and impressed with him that I smiled until my cheeks were hurting. He turned to me on the train and said you know when I find the right fit at one of these offices, you're not going to have to work so hard. In fact he told me I would be able to stay home and figure out what I really wanted to do with my life. He wanted to reward me time to find a career or build a business. This man never ceased to amaze me. He was such a dreamer and so selfless that all he wanted was to help me make my dreams and vision come true. I fell in love with Aaron over and over again everyday. Finally, we made it home that night from a wonderful and successful interview date. While attempting to wind down, he received a phone call from yet another company who he interviewed with earlier that day. The business was called Red Payments which was a merchant company. They expressed how impressed they were by him and they were inviting him to come back for a second interview. Which was no surprise because Aaron had the ability to talk his way in and out of ANYTHING. He could verbally go toe to toe with the best of them. His charm, sheer brilliance and wit was unmatched. The day came for his second interview, and he asked if I would accompany him once again. Of course I went along with him. My man asked for my support and he knew he had every bit of it.

He walked up to the doors of Red Payments and this is the part where he had to go alone. So I entertained myself by walking to Times Square and did a little window shopping and sightseeing. The interview went on for nearly 3 hours, and when he finally came down, I was standing right there. Eager to hear what happened and whether or not he got the position he interviewed for. He smiled a huge smile and said "I'm back baby! I got it!" He was no stranger to this type of work. He had worked a number of jobs as a broker; it was just something he had a passion for. A few years prior he had worked for a company called On Deck, where he worked his way up the corporate ladder quite quickly. Unfortunately, a chain of unfortunate events had taken place at that company, so by the time he and I had gotten together he was literally taking a break from life. On the way home we talked about the next steps we wanted to take as a couple and individually. Aaron wanted to eventually end up working in the financial district of Wall Street. He wanted to become a tycoon, a top leader who is powerful in the business world. in the big leagues; whereas, I had plans on making furniture and eventually owning my own shop.

Our goal as a couple was to move our children to a better environment. That was our bigger picture. The white picket fence, the fancy car and the grand wedding! Although we were still in our 3rd floor walk-up attic, we continued to make the best of it. We had our dreams all planned out and nothing was going to stop us, except one thing that was preventing our picture and vision from being perfect. As I mentioned before he has two daughters and I have one. We only had access to his oldest daughter and my daughter at that time. We were both smack dab right in the middle of separation from our spouses, and it seemed that our love came with a price: he wasn't allowed to see or speak to his youngest daughter. This was heartbreaking to witness, so I made the suggestion for him to attempt to reach out to his estranged wife. I needed Aaron to be whole on the journey that we were about to embark on. In an attempt to deal with the bitterness of his soon to be ex-wife, he felt like he wasn't making any progress with the situation at hand. She was trying to use their child as collateral damage. As sad as it was, I told him not to stop until she allowed him to visit. Finally realizing that she wasn't going to win, she gave in and decided to let Aaron see his daughter. Totally happy about it, he accepted the time that was offered, even if it were for just a short period. Aaron didn't care; he missed his daughter. He had never been away from her for this length of time. I was just happy that he was happy. He thanked me for encouraging him to fight for Cammie and being so understanding about the circumstances he had to face. My goal was to let him know that I had his back, and was in it for the long haul. Besides, I knew our little family wouldn't have been complete without Cammie.

The day came for us to pick up Cammie and he couldn't have been more nervous since he hadn't seen her in months. Aaron couldn't help but think what she was being told about the reason for his absence. Growing up with his father out of the picture for nearly his whole life, Aaron always strived to be the best father he could. Making sure these three little girls were understood was the assignment he was given in life. He crossed every "T" and dotted each "I". Lord knows it was a full-time job but he made sure he completed the task each and every day. Whether it was a phone call when they were with the other parent, or it meant rescuing them from boredom in our apartment. Or just having a conversation about random stuff like why cheese is yellow, why the sky is blue, or if the girls could get jobs at 6 years old (lol). Aaron made sure he entertained all of us.

Some months had passed and Aaron had started his position at Red Payments. He had been working his way up the ladder to move up in the company. Assuming he would start bringing in big checks, I was preparing to quit my job. Things had been going so well between us. Within these few months living together, we had taken a trip to Florida to see my brother and his family, which was amazing! We were spending time with all three of our children as a whole, not just our individual children. We had one child during one weekend, but the other two weren't around. Aaron and I went apartment hunting together. We were planning to get a new car with more space for all 5 of us to fit into comfortably, instead of my small two-door Honda Accord or his Kia Forte, which we ended up giving back to the dealership. We were well on our way to having the fairytale life that we had dreamed of. The best part about it is that we were building it together. We literally went from nothing to on our way to having everything we deserved. I had picked out a ring and 3 different wedding gowns in the matter of a few months. Aaron was such a dreamer as I mentioned before. He would plan to have things that most people would think are not tangible. He set his goals high as he walked out the door everyday with a plan to make a million dollars. He had entrepreneurial plans of starting his own company. He and his business partner and good friend Giovanni often had meetings on how to execute their plans for their company that would be named "Wolfpack Inc". Aaron loved the social structure and rules of conduct of how wolves operated in packs. No wolf was better than the other but everyone's role is important and vital to the family. Which is also why he wanted to create that as his family crest. So Aaron and Giovanni wanted to apply the same concept while building a strong foundation for Wolfpack Inc. After becoming a part of the Red Payments team, Aaron had decided to bring Giovanni on as well. With this tag team duo working side by side and a few little friendly competitions later, they would work their way up to being team leaders. In no time, the dynamic duo changed the office environment. Certain rules no longer applied, yet the duo rules were in full effect, and they became office favorites. Aaron and Giovanni caught the attention of the "higher ups" in very little time. In a matter of a short time his boss couldn't wait to show him off at the holiday party. The party had taken place a week before Christmas. Always being the life of the party Aaron just shined. Unfortunately, one of the office rules was no spouses or significant others were allowed at this party. I assume this was due to negative past incidents by some of the former associates was the reasoning behind that decision. So that meant that I had to stay home, which was fine because I had some time to myself. My daughter was with her father for the first half of her winter vacation, and both of his daughters were with their mothers. This also gave us a chance to miss one another since we have been inseparable since we moved in together. It also gave us the opportunity to prove the amount of trust we had between each other. He called me when he got to the event and a few times in between until his phone died. The last time he called I told him to go have fun. He responded with "I'm not here to have fun, I'm here to network and shake hands with the head of the company."

If I had any doubts or any mistrust for even a second, after he said that the thought was completely wiped from my thought process. He would always reassure me that no matter where he was in the world he would always come back to me. By the time the Christmas party was over, it had begun to rain and snow. It was about 12 midnight. I was in and out of sleep when I had received a call from a number that I didn't recognize. I answered and it was my love on the other end. He was letting me know that his phone had died, which I figured, and that he was on his way home. He told me how much he loved and missed me and that he couldn't wait to get home to me. Completely blushing and now awake, I turned the television back on and awaited his arrival.

About a half hour after speaking to him I received another phone call from the same number, only this time it was Aaron's colleague. Sounding as if he was very inebriated he asked if Aaron had made it home yet. I responded, "no not yet, but he called me from your phone not too long ago. He should be walking through the door any minute now." I was kind of worried for a moment and then remembered that the party was in the city and he and Gio were traveling by train. So anxious for him to get home I paced from the bedroom to the kitchen a few times. Finally I heard his keys opening the door, fifteen minutes after his colleague had called me. When he came in he was soaking wet and his hands were full. He had food in one hand and two big bottles in the other with an umbrella hanging on his wrist. Any feelings of worry that I felt quickly disappeared.

One bottle he bought was this expensive wine and the other was a tequila that I've never heard of before. He put everything on the counter and gave me the biggest hug and kiss as if we hadn't seen each other in months. He expressed as he grabbed my face that he needed me by his side next time. All I could do was smile. Not only did he come in with food and drinks but, he had a ton of stories! We ended up having a picnic in the middle of the kitchen and talked until about 3 in the morning. Those are the moments we lived for. We literally talked about everything. The next day he slept longer than usual. I figured it was because he had partied and because of our late night rendezvous in the kitchen afterwards. I let him sleep through the morning while I ran a few errands. When I returned home in the early afternoon he was still asleep. I woke him up as gently as possible because I was concerned. He usually beats me to the kitchen in the morning to cook breakfast. I asked him if he felt ok. He told me he didn't feel well at all. I touched his forehead and he was burning up. I looked at the collar of his shirt and it was drenched in sweat. I took his shirt off and replaced it with a dry one. Right away my motherly instincts kicked in. I gave him cold medicine, and cooked soup, and made sure he remained hydrated. I treated his sickness the way someone would treat the common cold. I administered medication, served ginger ale and fed him chicken noodle soup. *"You'll be back to feeling normal in no time"*, I thought. Sadly that was not the case this time. I let a couple days go by to see if Aaron's conditions would improve. He did not improve; in fact, his condition only got worse. Aaron's fever would come and pass. He was not eating--the only liquids he managed to drink was water as he sweated profusely through all of his clothes and all he wanted to do was sleep. He went through 3 ½ cases of water in just a few days by himself alone. This time I made the suggestion that he go to the hospital. He was not happy with the idea to say the least but, I made a deal with him. I said "let's give it one more day and if by tomorrow you don't get any better then I will take you to the ER." He gave as much of a smirk as he could muster up and we pinky promised. Pinky promises in our house held more merit than an actual promise. So the next day came and it seemed as if I hadn't seen his beautiful brown eyes in a week. I gave him until the late afternoon, on Christmas day to see if he felt any better. I couldn't even ask because he slept all day again. I woke him and told him time was up. I helped him get dressed and that was a process within itself. He was very lethargic, weak and burning up again with a fever. That's how I knew for sure it wasn't just a common cold. It had taken us quite some time to get out of the house. We finally made it to the hospital. This is where the circumstances of life truly put us through the test.

Our love broke barriers, especially the love for our children. As a parent I would often question If love was a strong enough expression of emotion. By being so confident, certain and exact about our love, we were able to take our honesty, respect, communication and things we believed our relationship to be, and pour it back into our children. We had done this with the intent that they would pass this frequency of love on to their own children. We didn't have much in our drafty third floor apartment but we had each other, just the five of us.

"Love isn't written in stone, here for a minute then gone.

Doll I'm not saying you don't, but I'm just sayin he won't.

Not strong enough to let go, he know you don't love him nomore,

But still he won't walk out the door.

So when it's time to move on, first it'll rain, it'll pour,

But I'm prepared for the storm.

It ain't nowhere I'm goin. And you know it.

I told you before, baby all you gotta do is endure.

This gonna be more than tug- a- war,

But I know what I'm doin. And you know it.

I've been through this before and I learned all is fair in love and war. Through the darkness, will guide you to dawn.

I know where I'm goin, it ain't nowhere I'm goin."

AARON HARVEY

CHAPTER 3
TOUGH PILL TO SWALLOW

When we arrived at the hospital, Aaron could barely hold his head up. So he laid on me as if I was his mama bear until he was called in the back to be screened and processed. After waiting about an hour, they called us in. The doctor finally came in and asked some basic questions. Then they had bloodwork done and administered several tests. The conclusion was drawn that Aaron had pneumonia. The nurse gave him albuterol treatment for a few minutes and some antibiotics. Skeptical of some of his symptoms, the doctor came in and asked a few more questions, then exited the room once more. As I looked at Aaron's face I could see him starting to come back to life, in a sense. He was talking more, and he didn't want to go back to sleep. He was awake and becoming very aware of his own body again. My mind was at ease knowing that the love of my life was going to be okay.

The doctor returned to the room with concerning news. He explained that Aaron was going to have to be transferred to another campus of the hospital because they were not equipped to treat the level of his needs in the ER. We both looked at each other with concern. This is where I realized that Aaron had struggled with extremely bad anxiety. I looked at him and held his hand and reassured him that everything was going to be fine. I told him that he's gonna be ok and that I was going to be there every step of the way. I pinky promised. The doctor probably just wanted to run more thorough tests to make sure it was just pneumonia. They carried him away into an ambulance and I followed behind in my car. On that long car ride I made a few phone calls to inform the people closest to us, and let them know that we were on our way to Summit, New Jersey. We arrived at this huge hospital and the nurses had him settled in a room and we still had no clue what was happening. They ran more tests and did more blood work still we had questions and they still had no answers. After being admitted, he spent a few days there. With really high fevers, they started to cause him to hallucinate. Aaron actually believed that he was at work everyday when in all actuality, he was in a hospital bed for several days now. It was really rough watching the man of my dreams lay sick in a hospital bed and not knowing what to do, and neither did the doctors. It was really frustrating for Aaron, and even though he began to gain a little more energy day by day, he was still sick and was growing weary of that hospital bed. The man was so clever that he started asking for ice packs from different nurses, and he placed them behind his back and neck to bring his fever down. He convinced the nurse to take his temperature, and his plan to leave the hospital by New Years day actually worked. I sat and watched as he literally broke free from this hospital by way of wit. They released him on New Year's day. So happy to be back home, he walked right to that kitchen window and began to reflect on the couple weeks that just passed by. Always considerate of my feelings, he asked how I was doing. I began to cry and expressed how scared I was because I hadn't seen his eyes or heard his voice in a week. Then we went from hospital to hospital and no one could give us answers as to why he was in the state that he was in. We hugged for a while by that window and just held on tight. A few days had passed since he'd been home and things were getting back to normal at *Harvey'z World.* Aaron was playing video games and I was preparing to go to the laundromat. Before I could make my way out the door Aaron's phone rang. It was the hospital making a follow-up call. The doctor asked him if he made an appointment with a doctor that he thought would be fitting for his condition. Aaron looked at me with a look of worry and said "no". The doctor told him how important it was for him to have his blood work done by this doctor because he was a specialist and he could help determine what was happening with him. Shortly after hanging up the phone Aaron called the specialist and made an appointment. The appointment was made for the day after. When we got to the office we had a little heated tiff with the receptionist. Aaron Harvey was not the type to tolerate disrespect but was always fair. So he corrected her on her attitude and misinformation and she apologized and so did he. As we waited in the sitting area, he seemed agitated and anxious. I caressed his back to ease his anxiety and started talking about music. Just to get his mind off of being in a doctor's office and the verbal exchange between him and the secretary.

He was finally called to the back, I stayed behind in the waiting area. After about 25 or 30 minutes had gone by he walked out to me and kissed me. He grabbed my hand and we left. The kiss wasn't anything out of the ordinary. That's how affectionate we always were.

It was the silence on the car ride home that made me think something was wrong. I asked if he was ok and he said "yeah babe, it's just not knowing that's killing me." I completely understood his position and allowed him to have a quiet moment to process everything. By the time we got home I had picked my daughter up. She was doing homework so we ate lunch, made some phone calls and played video games. As night time came I was about to cook dinner but had to run to the store first. As I'm walking around the store I kept getting a phone call from a weird number. The first 2 times I ignored it. I passed it off as a bill collector attempting to collect a debt. Then when the same number called the third time I answered. It was the doctor 's office that we had been to earlier. The doctor himself was calling and said that it was really important that he spoke to Aaron. So I dropped everything and ran back to the house. The store was only down the street from our house. I ran up three flights of stairs. Darted into the bedroom, trying to catch my breath to tell him to call the doctor right away. But before I could say anything he jumped up in worry as if he thought something happened to me. When I caught my breath I told him that the doctor had been trying to contact him for a while now. He couldn't reach him so he called me. Aaron grabbed his phone and saw that he had several missed calls. It turns out that he was so consumed with playing Call of Duty video game with his headphones on, that he didn't hear his phone ringing. Completely relieved knowing nothing was wrong because he still wasn't 100% better, I giggled and so did he. He had his phone in hand and was dialing the number back, but nothing at all could have prepared us for what happened next.

The phone rang and the receptionist picked up. Aaron asked to speak to the doctor. She put him on hold for a few seconds then the doctor picked up. He had the phone on speaker until the doctor picked it up. I gave him his privacy and walked into the kitchen to help my daughter with her homework and to start dinner. Aaron called me back into the room after a few seconds. He closed the door behind me and put the phone back on speaker. The doctor then proceeded to tell him that he may possibly have Leukemia. Aaron said in disbelief "you mean cancer?" The doctor confirmed and told him that he needed to get to Morristown Medical center right away. He told him that there was a bed waiting for him already. You could hear a pin drop in our bedroom. His face was so pale and he looked like he had seen a ghost and I immediately fell to pieces.

Cancer is a really tough pill to swallow. Everything we were building together to ensure a better life for us and our children had come to a screeching halt. Above anything else this man was the love of my life, my person, my soulmate, the one who I planned to spend forever with. I tried to put on a strong face for him but all I could do was cry as he held me in his arms. He was still in shock and was trying to process it all. He looked me in my eyes and told me that it was going to be ok. Only then I knew that my strength had to now be his strength, but right then he had to be strong for both of us. It was so automatic for us to try and lift one another up. Even with him knowing that he was about to face the toughest fight of his life. He still managed to display such power and control. I left the room trying to remain in one piece in front of my daughter. I knew he needed a minute to sort out his thoughts. He called his cousin Dante to pick him up and take him to the hospital since I had my daughter and he didn't want her to start asking questions. So I continued to cook as if nothing was wrong. Aaron continued or attempted to play video games. When Dante arrived he walked him into the bedroom and shut the door. My daughter, still doing homework, raised her head out of curiosity but said nothing. As the night went on, I dropped my daughter off at her father's house for the evening. I grabbed a few of our belongings and headed towards the hospital. Not knowing what was going to happen next and all kinds of thoughts and emotions running through my mind, I just drove and as I got closer to the hospital, I just prayed and prayed. I prayed that we just made it through this somehow or someway.

I arrived at the hospital to be by his side just as I promised. I had no clue what to expect or how he was feeling. Thinking if he was worried or scared, I continued to the elevator. I had butterflies in my stomach with fear of the unknown. To my surprise when I walked through the door I didn't expect to see what I saw. Aaron was there sharing jokes with the male nurse that was checking his vital signs. The look on his face was priceless when he saw me. He grinned from ear to ear as he introduced me as his fiance for the first time. Aaron had proposed to me a few times but because we couldn't afford a ring he just asked me for other things. The very first time was with a hatchet. He got down on one knee in this place called "Bury the Hatchet." This was one of our first dates just a few months prior and before he could even ask I said "Yes" about four times. One time he was empty-handed and I said 'yes'. I didn't care about the ring and neither did he. Nor did I think the first time he introduced me as his fiance would be to someone on the nursing staff in a hospital. I was just glad to see him in good spirits and acting like himself given the circumstances. We spent a day or two in the hospital before the doctors performed a bone marrow biopsy. This test was to determine if he really had leukemia and if so, how much there was. The day came for the results to be revealed to us. Aaron was nervous as to what the results would be but we stayed strong no matter the outcome. The doctor told us what could be expected moving forward before he told us the results. We were prepared for the worst, then the doctor said that Aaron in fact did have leukemia and that it was spreading fast. As bad as I wanted to cry I couldn't. I just reminded myself to be strong for him. We both took the news for what it was. In the middle of the conversation Aaron asked the doctor a number of questions. Without hesitation the doctor answered to the best of her ability. Aaron wanted to know the very questions that most cancer patients may be afraid to ask. He asked what his life expectancy was and that's when my ears had gone deaf. The entire conversation after that was a blur to me. I couldn't believe that death was even being discussed. Death and soulmate being mentioned in the same sentence just didn't seem real to me. I wasn't blind to the facts; it was just a very hard discussion to have after just spending five wonderful months together. And now having to face the music that my heart in human form may not be here to see our beautiful plan come to fruition.

CHAPTER 4
NIGHTMARE OF A DREAMER

Aaron had been in and out of hospitals most of our relationship. Being diagnosed with Acute Lymphoblastic Leukemia (ALL) just 6 months after we began dating, we were faced with some uncertainty that brought forth some of the hardest circumstances that we never thought we'd have to face, but for some reason we knew that as long we were together we could make it through anything.

From the outside looking in, people around us believed that we had the picture perfect love story. In fact we did, but that didn't stop anyone from questioning what was in the back of their minds. Especially some family members. Aaron and I had only been together for a short period of time. Then the ultimate life test happened, so they were all wondering if I was going to stick around and be by his side. Since preparing for death is a possibility and taking care of someone who is very ill is a huge responsibility. I was actually told that I could jump ship and move my things out of the apartment. I was completely offended because I never even hinted at the thought. I understand why I was presented with the option, but leaving was never a part of the plan. I had waited to be with this man since middle school and I absolutely was here to stay.

Being questioned by his ex-girlfriend about whether or not I had told this or that person that he was in the hospital was when I knew I had to make it clear to everyone that I wasn't letting him go. Having dealt with the skepticism of those closest to Aaron around us, I told myself I couldn't lose sight of the bigger picture. After having to put everyone in their place,the only thing I wanted to do was cuddle under Aaron to let him know that I was here forever--however long that was. His hospital stay became a very interesting one. People on the outside of his close circle were finding out the news about his condition. This included another lingering ex-girlfriend who thought it would be ok for her to visit. Aaron put a stop to the madness and didn't allow her to make her way to the hospital. Having to deal with a clingy ex who was also the mother of his oldest daughter, a lingering ex that just wouldn't go away and being told to jump ship probably should've all been deal breakers and a sign to let go. But nothing could match or compare to our connection and unbreakable bond. The entire situation really came down to a matter of trust. All of our cards were being put on the table.

I was still working, but slept at the hospital and traveled from there everyday. After work I would spend time with my daughter at her father's house. He would also be present and Aaron was not fond of the idea of me still being around my ex as often. I was left with very few choices and was exhausted both physically and emotionally. We were dealing with so many factors all at once and learning things about each other that we didn't know previously. Aaron's ex-wife put the icing on the cake. After learning of his illness, she took the opportunity to put him on child support. Things around us were unfolding and crumbling at a vast speed. Our dream of a grand wedding, moving and giving our children a better life was turning into a nightmare right before our eyes. It seemed like everyday it was something new happening that added weight to his condition. Aaron attempted to call his youngest daughter and he wasn't even allowed to speak to her. Instead, he was met with an argument between his estranged wife and her boyfriend who told Aaron that he should just die already. All Aaron wanted to do was explain to his daughter about his sickness himself and his ex-wife found a way to stop him. I couldn't stand by and watch him continue to fight a losing battle any longer without speaking to his daughter. He was already fighting the toughest battle for his life. So I tried to take his phone away from him to eliminate any further stress. He was so upset with the situation that he raised his voice at me and said "it's not about you", as if he thought that I was thinking that he wanted to talk to his ex for personal pleasure after the argument. Which wasn't the case at all. I left the room upset and in tears. I had never seen this side of him before. Again all of our cards were being shown. Whether we liked it or not, our relationship was being tested day by day, by the people closest to us. Trying to wrap my head around everything that just took place. I sat in the family room that was only next door to his room, separating the events that had just taken place. I allowed myself time to cool down before I walked back into the room. Not knowing what to expect next, I was willing to set our differences aside no matter what. Before I could say anything, surprisingly, he greeted me with a tight hug and a very sincere apology. I apologized also for not being clear about my intentions and explained why I tried to take the phone.

We understood where one another was coming from and was able to put our disagreement behind us. It was just that simple even though the situation itself was so complicated. We love each other unconditionally and it never took us long to get over a bad time. The amount of respect we had wouldn't allow it anyway. I missed him the second I walked out the door. While all of this was happening, Aaron's team of doctors were putting together a regiment and schedule for him to begin chemotherapy.

Everything was happening fast, but yet slow at the same time. Aaron was being monitored daily but still had to get things in order. The care team had to make sure that the regiment that was given would be effective against the type of leukemia that Aaron had, which was called Acute Lymphoblastic Leukemia (ALL). Not knowing what the next day would bring and in the midst of family and friends visiting, we had very little time to talk as much as we were used to. Things were changing and the clock was running. Realizing that time is a gift, we promised that we would make everyday beautiful. That meant no more arguments. Instead we talked and communicated lovingly to one another.

The time had come after being in the hospital for a few weeks for Aaron to begin chemotherapy. One of the nurses brought something to our attention that we hadn't even thought about. She asked if we planned on having more children. Without any hesitation we both said "yes" in unison. We had our future son's name picked out before we even had sex. But ever since Aaron had been in the hospital, so much was happening that the thought never occurred. She explained that chemotherapy may prevent that from happening in the future. All of the chemicals that he would have pumped into his bloodstream was going to make him sterile. So, she advised us to consult with a sperm bank. We did just that, and found a nearby medical center that could supply us with the proper storage utensils. Luckily it was directly across the street from the hospital. I ran smack dead in the middle of winter across a four lane highway just to grab what he needed. There was no transportation available to pick up the specimen so I was instructed to put it under my coat to contain as much heat as possible and drive it directly to the sperm bank in Mountainside which was about a twenty minute drive from the hospital. I did exactly as instructed, but I had absolutely no clue where I was going. My GPS had taken me on a wild crazy goose chase. I remember breaking down crying on my way there. The fact that we couldn't do things the natural way was devastating and heartbreaking to me. I did not allow those thoughts to consume me for long. I slapped my superwoman "S" on my chest and continued to my destination. I had a conversation with myself about the fact that no matter the outcome, Aaron and I would still have our little boy. This was just an alternative and a precautionary measure.

I cried a lot during the early stages of Aaron's treatment. I cried in my car because I refused to let him see me sad. I wasn't sad because I thought he would die, but because he meant the world to me, and it hurt to see him have to go through so much all at once. It just seemed so unfair that not only did he have to be poked and prodded on a regular basis, but also dealing with challenges and drama in all other areas of his life.The only thing that kept me hopeful was how much energy he still had. Aaron actually became very popular on the oncology wing of the hospital. He was literally being asked to speak to other patients just to spread some of his positive attitude around. When I would get to the hospital from work each night we would go for a walk. He would make sure he had some Lorna Doone cookies and ginger ale waiting for me when I got there. Then he would grab his IV pole that he was hooked up to and we would talk and joke down the hallway.

By this time Aaron had been visited by the hospital's psychologist named Dr. White. Dr. White and Aaron became acquainted very quickly. They would talk and share laughs quite often. Aaron was dealing with many different emotions as one could imagine. One day while I was at work Aaron called and told me that they had switched his room. I asked why? He told me about a conversation between him and Dr. White had prior to him calling me. He said that Dr. White asked if there was anything he could do for him. Aaron said jokingly,"Yes you can get me a room with more damn windows." The room he was in only had one window and being that we were both just over 5 feet, we had to get a chair to look out of it. We both liked scenery and only had the view of a back entrance. By the time I got to the hospital, Aaron was moved to the corner room. It had a lot of windows and a front view of the hospital. On the other side there was a full view of the helipad. Talk about an upgrade. When I visited, we saw some of the most beautiful sunsets from those windows. We would put the hospital bed up as high as we could get it and just watch the sky change colors as it set behind the mountains in the distance. Some days he would fall asleep while laying on me and I would sing to him while we took in the sights. Although cancer was a tough pill to swallow, it made us closer and stronger as a unit. I didn't know how strong I actually was until I had to be strong for him.

As the days went by Aaron was well into his chemotherapy treatments, he began to feel all the side effects that the care team had mentioned he would start to feel. The one he least expected to feel actually became the worst for him. As I walked in from work, I was anticipating our walk down the hallway. I saw him just sitting on the side of the bed with his head down. I was always excited to see what his reaction would be when I walked in the door. I was usually greeted with a huge smile and open arms with him being ready to hold my hand until we made our way to the nurse's station. He was so happy and anxious to see me come back to him each evening. This evening the aura was very different. I dropped everything that I was carrying and I stood in front of him and lifted his head. All I saw were tears. I asked him what was wrong. He explained how he couldn't take two steps without feeling winded and seeing stars. The look of devastation and defeat was written all over his face.

This was a person who took pride in still being able to do back flips and sprinting down the street well into his 30's. So not being able to simply walk was catastrophic to him. In fear that I wouldn't know what to say, I stood quiet for a few seconds and held him as he cried. I wanted to cry with him but there was a force within me that wouldn't allow it. As I held in my anguish, I lifted his head once more and said "hey, it's only temporary. You're so strong here and in there", as I pointed to his head and his heart.

He dried his eyes and hugged me tightly. I hugged him just as tight and this time I think I put all of his broken pieces back together. I told him "this is gonna be a rough journey and I'm not going anywhere." I wanted him to know that he wouldn't be doing it alone, and that I wasn't gonna be easy on him either. He smirked at me. Until this very day, I could only think that by the grace of God was the only way I could've ever displayed that much strength. He still wanted to go out into the hall for his daily walk with me. I excused myself for a second and went into the bathroom and cried for him. Of course I didn't want him to see so I washed my face and walked back into the room and helped him out of bed. We didn't make it very far but he did his best and that's all I could've ever asked. I was so proud that he even tried.

The more he walked each day the more he gained his strength back. He never gave up and pushed himself until he was able to make it all the way to the family room at the other end of the hall. He went in to make himself some tea. I stayed behind to clean up the room. While in the process of adding the accoutrements to his tea. He couldn't help but overhear a father and son discussing the mental and emotional state of his other son who was also fighting some form of cancer. Aaron couldn't help but intervene. He approached the family members of this young man and asked if he could speak to him. Completely in shock at the current state that he appeared to be in, with his IV pole in one hand, and cup of tea in the other. There were wires coming from underneath the armpit of his hospital gown. They looked at each other then looked at Aaron, and told him that if he thinks he can help in any way then they'd welcome him. They both agreed to have him come into the room. They shook hands as they introduced themselves. They gave Aaron the room number and asked that he come by after a certain time. Only because the young man would be going for physical therapy. When Aaron returned to the room he told me what had just taken place. I smiled and told him how proud I was of him for having the courage and guts to even make the suggestion. That's how selfless he was; he would actually go and help someone else by being positive during the fight of their life as he's fighting for his very own life. I really couldn't have been more proud.

The time came for Aaron to go to the young man's room. He walked in, with me standing right beside him. His room looked exactly the way Aaron's when we first arrived there. Family members lined up against the wall. Aaron stood right in front of the bed and introduced himself and so did the young man. His name was Kyle. Kyle was just a tad bit younger than Aaron. Aaron told him his story and how he ended up in the oncology unit. He told him not to give up. Aaron instructed Kyle to call his room when he was able to walk so they could walk together. Aaron said that if Kyle didn't call, then he would come and stalk his room. Everyone in the room laughed, but the only laugh that counted in that room to Aaron was Kyle's. He was still a bit weak so he couldn't give much movement but he let out a little giggle. By the time we left that room we all had tears in our eyes. The father and brother that Aaron had just met in the family room couldn't have been more thankful and grateful for what he had just done for Kyle. He had changed that family's entire outlook on the situation. He gave Kyle more courage to use in his fight. As we made our way back to our room I just looked at him in amazement. With him being in for the fight of his life this man just kept making me fall in love with him more and more each day. Just having tears in his eyes not too long before because he himself couldn't walk but found it in him somehow and somewhere to help someone else was just so damn incredible to me. He was walking on air after realizing what he had done for the Mitchels, yet knowing that the hard part was still yet to come for the Harveys. Aaron hadn't seen his children for a while, which was weighing on us both. So Grace's mom had brought her to see Aaron. Grace is just as smart as her father, so she had so many questions. Quick on his feet as usual, he explained the best way he could about exactly what was happening and how the doctors were helping him stay alive. He provided her some comfort with the answers he gave her. She had just turned 10 years old at the time, but with the mind capacity of a teenager. Even though she understood more than we liked, he still explained it to her in the sense of a 10 year old. The hardest part for him came when he tried explaining it to our 5 year olds over the phone. He muscled through until they were satisfied with the answers.

Watching him melt over these 3 little girls made me realize that we were tougher than cancer. The foundation we were beginning to build was still standing very strong and impenetrable.

CHAPTER 5
REASSURING

In any relationship reassurance is an important factor. Especially, With all of the temptation in the outside world.With me being at work all day while he was in the hospital created some insecurities. I worked around a lot of men. My line of work was considered to be a man's job. Although, there were other women who worked alongside me. None of them hardly spoke english. I was popular at my job because for a woman I drove better than most of the men there. Aaron knew this and with him feeling the way that he did while being in his current condition made him a little uneasy.

I would call him so many times during the day, and he would call me. Then I would call on my lunch break, 15 minute break and I would sneak calls in the bathroom in between. He appreciated it so much.

Also dealing with depression and just having so many doubts and fears of what the future held, I made sure he knew that he was the only man that I wanted. I don't care if I had to drill that in his head every minute of every day. He was the only one that occupied so much space in my mind. Neither of us had ever been in this type of situation before. We were literally learning as we went along. We didn't see cancer in the forecast of our love story. It definitely had taken some getting used to. From my work schedule to stopping to spend time with my daughter, and making sure his mental state was ok day to day was a challenge but eventually just became the norm. We made it look easy and effortless.

We were having way more ups than downs. Aaron was in the middle of his chemotherapy regimen, and he had just a few weeks left of his hospital stay. On schedule and having already been there for over a month, it was still freezing cold outside but spring was approaching just around the corner. We were ready to be back at *Harvey'z World.* The nursing staff had become extended family and his room had a revolving door. Some of the nurses would come to visit even if they didn't have him as a patient that day. Morristown Medical offered so many amenities such as massage therapy, pet therapy, art therapy and regular therapy. I actually witnessed him offer one of the therapists personal therapy. Sometimes the therapists would argue in the hall over who was next to come in the room. Aaron even became friends with one of the technicians on the floor. He actually came to the hospital on his day off, during halftime of the superbowl with a whole bunch of food. A few of Aaron's friends had also stopped by. He had a superbowl party without having to ever leave his room.

It was so amazing to watch how much love others had for Aaron. Kyle would visit from time to time to play video games and to simply just talk. So it wasn't too bad. We just really missed being home. Aaron and I cherish the quiet moments like one Saturday when we stayed in the room all day watching movies and binge watching our favorite shows. We decided it was time for our stroll with me, him and his IV pole. As we walked down the hallway, a man's voice came from one of the rooms. We both looked up as he began to speak. He said "hey, are you Aaron Harvey?" We looked at each other. Then Aaron responded hesitantly "yeah". He came out from behind the door a little more and we could see his long wavy hair, tall stature and pale skin. He introduced himself while presenting Aaron with a business card. He explained how he heard a lot about him around the oncology unit and how he was the most positive patient and wanted to chat with him.

The man went back into the room and we continued on our walk.

We smiled at each other and laughed and said, "ok that was weird and cool." Aaron read the card and was shocked to know that this person was actually an engineer for a rapper that we grew up listening to. Completely in awe that word was getting around that he was serving a purpose and changing lives in the midst of his own battle was something to be proud of. The next day Aaron had reached out to him. They talked for some time and of course he was invited into the room. He formerly introduced himself to me as Josh. It was like the universe placed Josh there at the perfect time. Aaron needed to focus his mind on something other than his own circumstances. Josh wasn't a patient. In fact his girlfriend Latiesha was. She had been a patient there for a while also and was being treated for lymphoma. Come to find out, the doctor and nurses had been trying to get us all to meet. We were so happy to have met Josh and Latiesha even though it was under these circumstances. It was just so refreshing to have another couple to talk to while walking on this path. We dealt with some of the similar situations in our relationships. We would share stories and laughs about our journeys both in and out of the hospital. The time that we all spent together was therapeutic for all of us. Aaron and Latiesha were doing the hardest part, while Josh and I were there to be their strength on their toughest and darkest days.

Never in a million years did any of us ever think we would be in this situation, but it was reassuring that everything we were experiencing in our love life at that time was normal. We were not the only ones going through it. Our friendship with this beautiful couple began to blossom to the point where Aaron felt comfortable enough to perform for Josh right from his hospital bed.

He had written this song called "I don't apologize." This is actually one of my favorite songs! Keep in mind that Aaron was still having trouble with his breathing at times due to the amount of chemotherapy he was receiving daily. I watched as he sat straight up and took a few deep breaths. He looked at me and I looked at him with the look of question on my face wondering if he would be able to keep up with his breath in between the lyrics. He took a few more deep breaths and said " ok, here we go." I was so worried that he would be so winded. As difficult as it was to breathe he muscled through, giving background ad-libs and everything.

Josh was so impressed with his rapping abilities that they actually devised a plan to record the song bedside. I was still flabbergasted at the fact that he found the inner strength to do what he does best. They never got around to recording in the hospital but that didn't stop us from getting together. Josh's job required him to travel. So, some days Latiesha would be alone. That was until I would pop up in her room while Aaron napped. We bonded so well, she was always in such good spirits.

We talked about our wonderful men and families and how our individual loads that we carried at one point in time seemed so much lighter than when we met each other. Me and Aaron were so excited to have met them. We would bask in the fact that they are "our" friends, not people that he knew previously.

Caring for someone who has cancer is an around the clock job. There is so much to care for and the job requirements are not just making sure that person takes their medicine or how much chemotherapy they have to tolerate. While those things are important as well, it's also about keeping your loved one positive when they feel like giving up. It's about making them feel as comfortable as possible. You have to also take care of the inner parts; parts that matter most and they trust no one else with those vulnerable parts but you. The mind, heart, and spirit and catering to each of these needs is a job within itself. The strongest part of any human being is the mind. The power of strength and sheer will power starts in the mind. Fighting cancer is a tough battle, but is no match for the strong willed.

Keeping Aaron's mind positive comes easy to me. He and I are a lot alike so oftentimes music is the cure. I'm always so intrigued to find him listening to the most diverse playlist. His ear for music is so amazing. He listens to everything from Gershwin's "Rhapsody in Blue", to the Red Hot Chilli Peppers band, Billy Joel, and Wintergatan in short moments. The next minute Aaron listened to 6lack, J-Cole, Mick Jenkins, and Nipsey Hussle just to name a few.

He is the most fascinating man I've ever known and I fall in love with him everyday. So if it takes an entire day for me to reassure him, then I'm here forever and will do whatever it takes to ensure his comfort.

SECTION TWO

CHAPTER 6
BACK ON TRACK

Adjusting to home life is a little more challenging than I expected. After spending most of the winter of 2018 and some holidays in the hospital, we finally made it home by St. Patrick's Day. The hospital walls and nurses' station were decorated with shamrocks, rainbows and leprechauns. While we waited for the release forms, me and Aaron's brother Horacio packed up the cars. It seems as if we had moved our entire apartment into this hospital room. We had the game console,a bed topper, food, clothes and whatever else that could be found in our actual apartment. Aaron's comfort meant everything to me. His every wish was my command.

While Horacio and I did the heavy lifting, Aaron was changing his clothes to make his grand exit from the oncology wing. Aaron's mother had bought him a Hugh Hefner costume especially for this occasion. The costume consisted of a sailor's hat, a red smoker's jacket, and a pipe. Aaron looked too adorable in it. Horacio and I helped him take his final steps toward freedom. He was still weak and could walk on his own, but we helped with the first few steps. He stopped at the nurses' station to bid his farewells to some of the nurses who had been taking very good care of him. They could not believe how he really strutted his stuff down the hallways in style. They loved his personality and how true he stayed to himself throughout his fight with Leukemia. They especially loved the way he was kind enough to help others.They clapped for him and hugged him and gave their well wishes. I thought I was going to have to prye one nurse off with a crowbar.

We didn't know what to expect when we returned home even though I was still coming home from time to time to grab clothes and other things that Aaron asked me to bring to the hospital. The apartment was desolate and you can definitely tell that no one had been here for a while. The smell of wood was present instead of the scents of food, and our personal fragrances of perfumes and cologne.

Horacio stayed for a few minutes and helped bring everything inside. It was beginning to snow outside, it seemed like spring just didn't want to come around. It was slippery so Horacio had to help Aaron up the stairs. As carefully as he could and being winded after every step, he finally made it upstairs. After sitting down and getting settled, I realized that our floors have no molding on them. We are already missing the molding on our doorways and now we have none on the floors again. Our landlord was known for cutting corners. So he took our molding that he just installed a few weeks ago and put it in the apartment below us. We didn't let it bother us one bit. We had bigger fish to fry and we were just so happy to be in the place we called home--*Harvey'z World.*

Aaron walked around the apartment, and went into each room. First the bedroom, next the girl's room, then into the bathroom, and went directly to the kitchen window. He looked into the backyard briefly and had to sit down. He was still exhausted from the walk up three flights of stairs. So he had to go and lay down. He was too excited and restless to sleep so he just figured he'd play video games. That didn't last long either. I laid next to him after he turned off the game. He cuddled under me and we just laid there and reflected. I said, "babe! broooo! you just beat cancer's ass!" He smiled at me with that huge grin and said, "nigga I know! It's so crazy to even hear you say that to me." Then I asked if we could go to Disney world. We laughed so hard at our own conversation until finally falling asleep.

He was still on the hospital schedule so he wanted to sleep a lot. By the next morning he woke up early and he wanted to drive to the Pier which was 5 minutes down the road. The wind was blowing as we approached the water. He closed his eyes and breathed deep and took it all in. These are the little things in life that we take for granted. Not being able to feel the wind on his face or smell the outdoors made him appreciate that moment so much more. Aaron took a moment to smell the roses life had just recently offered him. By midday our phones were ringing with calls from family members from all over. From His Italian family in Ohio to his mother's family members that live in Georgia. My mother, sisters and my brother that lives in Florida and our daughters also gave us a call. It really warmed our hearts to see the outpour of love from our families. He saved the last call for his cousin Mike. Mike and Aaron have the best relationship I've ever seen anyone have between cousins. Aaron was always the one giving everyone advice about everything. Mike was the one Aaron went to for advice. I tell him all the time how happy I am that he has Mike. They are both highly intelligent and knowledgeable about everything, so those conversations could go on for hours.

While he conversed with his cousin, it gave me a chance to have some alone time. Just taking a quiet moment in between to just breathe. This helped me to keep my sanity. I did some reflecting myself. I just couldn't believe what we had just gone through for the past two months. We survived people trying to break us up, survived our own doubts and fears of our relationship, and most importantly, we survived cancer together!

We survived where most relationships would have failed. Feeling like a new woman because the love of my life had returned home with me, I decided to cook a special meal. His welcome home dinner was steak, mashed potatoes, and green beans. When I brought him his plate he had the biggest smile on his face. I put the plate down and he grabbed me and pulled me into his lap and kissed me. He thanked me for everything on a regular basis but this "thank you" was different.

He was teary eyed as he lovingly told me how much he appreciated me for being there. He made me cry as he expressed his gratitude for me not leaving his side despite all the craziness. He always knows how to make me get all emotional. Just a simple 'thank you' made me want to give him the world. I explained to him how he made it easy. If I had listened to all the outside noise of exes and family members, I would be the one losing out.

It was now the beginning of April and things in the Harvey household were getting back on track. Aaron's immune system was getting stronger and we were able to have company. We would have the girls more frequently. We began to pick up right where we left off. There were still frequent doctor visits and monitoring happening daily, but we were living. Aaron asked me if I was still going to marry him. I said without a doubt or hesitation 'yes.' So we had some planning to do, on top of that we were apartment hunting again.

Looking for more space that would be comfortable and affordable for all five of us was a doozy some days; we had our work cut out for us, but stress was not an option especially in Aaron's case. I prayed and prayed that we would find something suitable for our living needs. My prayers went unanswered. I figured there had to be a reason why the hunt for a bigger apartment left us hopeless. Not realizing that there were more holidays approaching and birthdays, I had to save money anyway.

I was the only one working again so it was hard trying to balance bills, birthdays and fun time expenses. The good thing about it is that it was starting to get nice outside and we were able to be outdoors more. The parks were not far from our house. Thank God for that because that's where we spent a lot of time with the girls. All of our birthdays were consecutively back to back. We only got a little break in between Aaron and Skylar's birthdays. Literally from April to June then to September we were broke with very little cash. As I said before, money never limits our chances at having fun.

Aaron wanted to help lighten the load, so he pushed himself to go back to work. I protested because I thought it was too soon. He had just been released from the hospital just a few days shy of a month ago. Knowing how strong his will and determination is, I caved in and agreed. I sat and watched as he meticulously picked out his clothes. He actually wore the same thing that he wore to the holiday party. He made the comment about what he was wearing and said, "I just want to pick up where I left off."

I stayed home from work just in case he needed me for anything. It was still cold outside so I went ahead and warmed up the car for him. While sitting in the car I said a little prayer for him to make it to and through the day at work, still on the fence about letting him go into work. When we arrived at the train station I asked him one more time if he was sure he wanted to go in.I explained to him numerous times that I could continue to hold us down. He looked at me, gave me a kiss and said yes. So I sat in the car and watched him walk to catch the train. As soon as I pulled away, my eyes welled up with tears.I wasn't upset but emotional and proud. I don't know what I did in life to deserve such a man. To watch him be so strong to fight through everything he just faced, to now get up out of bed and push forward with such stride and pure determination in his eyes. Just wanting to provide for me and those girls was sexy, inspiring and motivating. Even though he didn't make it through the work day, his efforts were not in vain. He called me to meet him at the train station maybe an hour after getting there. I must admit I was so relieved. His boss wouldn't allow him to push himself as hard as he did. So he sent him back home. But not before telling him how he will always have a desk waiting for him. Aaron's boss just wanted him to recover and heal. I will forever be grateful for him. It was so incredible to watch.

Aaron thinks of himself as a superhero. He truly has incredible abilities that I admire so much. Anything and everything was possible to him. Whether it's actually possible or not, Aaron always believes the impossible could be done. Nothing was ever impossible to this man. He actually ran into a burning building to save an old lady a year or two prior to us dating. How impressive is that?! Whenever he was told he couldn't do something, he would show the naysayers and haters how he could do it and just how well it can be done. He felt that in the corporate world he identified with "The Green Lantern" for his own reasons, but to me and the girls he is definitely Superman.

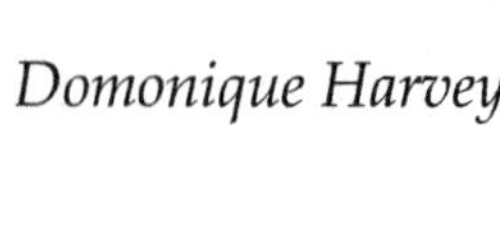

"Be strong , Be fearless, Be beautiful. And believe that Anything is possible when you have the right people there to support you."

MISTY COPELAND

CHAPTER 7
THE RELAPSE

As human beings we know that healing takes time. Allowing the body time to recover and repair itself requires plenty of rest. Except when your name is Aaron Harvey. Although he couldn't participate in too many outdoor activities due to his fluctuating white blood cell count, he found ways to stay active indoors. It wasn't hard with our three leading ladies Grace, Cam and Sky. For Easter we dyed eggs with the girls and periodically did a bunch of paintings and drawings to hang up around the house. We would do things to keep them busy but in all actuality they were keeping us on our toes.

As the seasons changed so did the holidays and birthdays. In April and May we celebrated Grace, Cam's and my birthday and Mother's Day. Grace turned 11 and Cam and Sky turned 6 even though Sky's birthday wasn't until September. In June we celebrated Aaron's birthday and Father's Day. For Aaron's birthday we actually added a new member to our family. Aaron's cousin Camille had gifted him a dog. She was a little white chihuahua mixed with another breed. We named her "Cleo" and she fit right in.

In July our anniversary rolled around and he was feeling great most days. I wanted to celebrate him beating cancer when he was well enough to actually enjoy the festivities, and not having to worry about everyone's germs being hazardous to his health. I planned to surprise him with a dinner celebration to celebrate life. Wracking my brain trying to figure it all out by myself, because it seems like everyone was too busy living their best lives, so that just left me. I didn't mind doing it alone . Going online just about everyday looking for decorations. Looking for the right venue and getting a guest list together is a hard task but it was fun. It's hard to keep a secret from him, because he knows me so well and knows if I'm hiding something. It could be the simplest thing that would give it away. The way I smile or the way I would constantly be checking my phone. Around him I usually forget that I own a phone.

There was no way in the world that I could pull it off. He saw right through me. So instead of a party, he asked if we would just use the money that we saved to go away. I went on the internet and researched fun things to do near New Jersey. The second suggestion that popped up was zip lining in Pennsylvania. He was all for a fun adventure in the trees! He had never been and I haven't been since high school. After it was decided what to do, we then researched where to stay. The closest place we could find next to the facility where the zip lining would take place was called "Rainbow Mountain." We were impressed with all of the amenities that this place had to offer. The reservations were made for that following week and away we went!

As we drove to our hotel we had an incredible time. The moment we got in the car, music was blasting and we were full of smiles. We were so excited to be celebrating just the two of us. No headache of a guest list or overpaying for a venue. Just us, as it has been for the past year! We planned to *"put one in the air"* as we crossed state lines form New Jersey to Pennsylvania. Then we went back and forth telling each other why we love each other as much as we do. Not to compare or to measure but the *WHY* of it all. I expressed how glad I am to be born in this moment and time, with him. Arriving at Rainbow Mountain we were high as a kite. We got into the lobby to check in and were both looking around at the pictures on the wall and the people coming in and out. As we waited for the clerk to return to the front desk we were also starting to notice there were international flags hanging up just outside of the door as they hung very neatly and nicely to give more flair to the decor.

We checked in and made it to our room. The room and surrounding view of this place was breathtaking. We were in the middle of the woods. All that could be heard was the natural sounds of birds chirping and the sound of our love making in the greater outdoors. Much like a newly married couple we just couldn't keep our hands off of each other. And the atmosphere just created the most romantic aura. Even though our surroundings never really mattered. We had a lot of lost time to make up for. Being that we felt that we were running late within our relationship. We lived out our teenage fantasy in one weekend. We barely came out for air that first night until we got hungry. As soon as the bags hit the floor, so did our clothes. We began kissing and smiling and talking while we kissed. In between we were undressing each other. Both bursting with passion, we lost all control as he laid me on the bed. I continued to feel his nature rise. After the third round of wild untamed sex and some cuddling, we finally came outside and hung out around the tennis court and took a little quiet nature walk to absorb all the sights this place had to offer before dinner. There was a restaurant that connected to the lobby and we decided we would eat there instead of getting back into the car and driving into town. We had taken showers and changed into our night wear. We loved to coordinate our outfits. Wearing all white, we walked down the long hallway to the front door. As we walked across the street to the restaurant, there was a man walking past us wearing chap pants that revealed his butt, and holding hands with another man. Totally caught off guard, me and Aaron looked at each other in complete shock. Not that we cared about them holding hands, but it was the fact that we were in a place where this man was allowed to wear his ass out in public. We snickered to ourselves as we were so confused as to why he had his butt hanging out for all to see. Thinking back to when we first walked in, one of the flags that hung out front was a rainbow flag, which is considered to be a symbol of lebian, gay, transgender and queer pride social movements.

We were so stoned and completely high when we first arrived that we bypassed every sign that would indicate that this was a gay resort. There was also no mention of that small detail on their website. We laughed so hard at how we ended up here. Completely unbothered by it because Aaron's mother is also a part of the LGBT community and we simply don't care about anyone's sexul preference. But, she later revealed that she too had spent time there before. She asked about our trip and we told her where we stayed. Her response was. "What were yall doing there?! That's one of my spots!" We shared a good laugh after we told her the story.

We continued on with our night. Afterwards, we ate and drank and then heard really loud music coming from the bottom of the hill of the resort. We followed the tunes into what looked like a nightclub. We soon found out why the man we saw just before dinner was wearing those chaps with his butt out. We saw way more wacky and interesting "get ups" than his. People were walking around with whips, chains, and while some were being walked on dog leashes. The night was young so we did what we do best and lived in the moment. We drank a little more before participating in karaoke night. We even made new friends with a few gay couples. Our time spent there was definitely one for the books. No one judged anyone and we were all able to exist in one place and just enjoy each other's company comfortably. It was definitely a night that we will both remember.

The next day we went zip lining and had the most amazing time. It was a two hour course and we were running late. We overslept then got lost on the way there, even though it was only 15 minutes away from our resort. When we got there we were met by an instructor who gave us a crash course on how the equipment works. The group that we were supposed to be a part of had gone ahead, so we were led to a golf cart with Monster tires on it. The man driving told us to hold on tight. We did just that as he instructed as he seemed to be going at top speed up a mountain of rocks. I literally thought that we were going to tip over, but it didn't stop us from whipping out our phones and taking videos and pictures. While climbing up trees and crawling through nets, Aaron made sure he took the opportunity to just be in the moment with me.

He looked at me as we reached the top of a tree and said "this is fun babe. I never thought I'd have anyone to do this with." I blushed and felt as if he was cheated this entire time. Out of all the women he has dated it was kind of hard to believe. Then again he lived multiple lifestyles and didn't have time to climb trees. Besides, I think I was the one he was waiting for to fill these voids. Our weekend of fun was coming to an end and we didn't want it to be over. We wished we could do that on a regular basis. Returning home we reflected on life. Realizing that because he was still getting used to this new way of life due to cancer, we had to get back to reality, which was doctor visits and chemotherapy. Only this round of chemo he would have to stay in the hospital a few days at a time. After some chemo sessions he would be really sick. Other days he was just really tired. Some days it even put him in a really bad mood. Those were days we gave each other space. Unless he just wanted me to be present but even still I would be silent and just lay with him on his hospital bed. My presence granted him peace as he did the same for me.

We operated this way until about four months later in November. Aaron was beginning to feel better again. Finding his inner strength to muscle through treatment did him some good because his health was improving. He was able to run again without losing his breath and chase the girls around. Christmas was the following month and I was secretly shopping for him. I asked what he wanted, and he literally said nothing. So grateful to just be alive was good enough for him. He never really asked for much anyway. The idea finally came to me on what to get him.

Aaron has a need for speed. He literally would ride or drive anything with wheels. He had told me about this thing called A One Wheel months ago. It was almost like a skateboard but it only had one big wheel in the middle and it was motorized. I looked at the price tag on it and figured there was no way I could afford that thing. It was almost $1000.00! Let's just face it, after rent , bills, and birthdays and our celebration of life, I just didn't have that kind of money laying around. I did a little more research and saw a "pay as you go"option at the bottom. They did a credit check and boom, I was approved. There was an email sent with the delivery details. Trying to contain my excitement because I didn't want to give it away like I did the surprise celebration, I walked in the bathroom and jumped for joy! I knew he was going to flip out when he saw it.

I had no idea where all these blessings were coming from, but I was glad that God and the universe continued to conspire to work in our favor. Having good credit didn't hurt either. The day came for his gift to be delivered and I ran into another issue. I couldn't figure out where to hide it in the house. It was a very expensive gift so I was not trusting it in the hands of anyone. I decided to just give it to him that day--a month before Christmas. I set it up in the kitchen with no imagery on the boxes and covered them with a sheet and called him to come out of the bedroom. He came out and had no idea what to expect. He said with the cheesiest grin on his face "what's this babe? Two midgets fighting in a wrestling ring?" I was not ready for that comment. I laughed until I couldn't breathe. He finally opened the huge boxes and he was so surprised and speechless. He ran through the house with excitement. He came and gave me the biggest hug and a million and one kisses.

He rode it around the house until he was able to ride it outside. The ground was wet because it had rained and snowed earlier that morning. I loved seeing him happy. Especially with all the pain he had endured. Like a kid in the candy store, he was so excited. He used this thing as if it were a regular vehicle. He went to the store on it. He would choose that One Wheel everyday before he drove a car.

One day in January, I was at work and received a call from him. He called prior to leaving the house and said he had to go to the social security office. I wanted to send him in an Uber but he chose to ride that one wheel. I pleaded with him to be careful, regretting every moment that I didn't get him any safety gear. By the time he decided to go to his appointment at the social security office it was almost time for me to come home from work.

We arrived home at the same time and after watching a little bit of television he decided to tell me that he fell earlier. I immediately jumped up and began examining him. Starting from his head and then pulling up his shirt while asking if he was hurt. He giggled at the way I showed concern. He showed me exactly where he fell on his left side. There was no bruising but there were a few red dots that resembled a scrape, but we thought nothing of it. Two days later he began to complain about a cramping feeling on the same side he had fallen on.

We took no chances and made a trip to the Morristown emergency room. Since Aaron was already being treated there, he was under special care instructions. Once again, around the holiday season we found ourselves in the ER. Experiencing being seen by a doctor seemed like a bad case of deja vu. I couldn't help but blame myself. If I hadn't bought that onewheel this wouldn't have happened. Just as the year before, there were all kinds of tests being run. X-Rays finally came about and it shows that he had a partially collapsed lung.Any hope of him leaving the hospital that night had gone right out the window at that point. They actually had orders to admit him into the hospital. I felt so guilty that I was the reason he was laying in this hospital bed yet again.

We knew the route by now and could navigate through this hospital with our eyes closed. The doctor explained that he would be moved back to the oncology unit for further testing. While looking over Aaron's chart he wanted to make sure that the leukemia wasn't coming back. All the nurses were astounded to see that we had returned. It was a somber walk down those hospital hallways. The next day there were doctors and nurses in and out of his room. No one had answers, very much like our very first trip to the ER a year earlier. We waited patiently because unlike the first time, we knew we were in good hands. We just had to allow them to work and examine all test results. Finally the doctor had ordered for Aaron to have several more tests done, including a bone marrow biopsy. A bone marrow biopsy involves removing a small piece of bone marrow inside your bones for testing. It's a soft tissue in the middle of large bones and makes up most of the body's blood cells. This would help determine if the leukemia had returned and how much there might be.

Days were going by and Aaron's condition was getting worse. He would bruise so easily after being poked with a needle or just a hard touch of the hand, which isn't normal for him. After having the biopsy done we awaited the results and sure enough it was as they suspected--the leukemia had returned. He had relapsed and although I felt bad that he fell off his onewheel, it was actually what saved his life. So it was a good thing because they were able to catch the cancer before it could do more damage, they thought. Aaron began having nose bleeds and his organs were beginning to shut down. His liver was enlarged and his lungs were not in good condition either. Soon he needed to wear an oxygen mask at all times. His eyes were jaundiced and he had bruises everywhere. Blowing his nose became a horrible task as well. He would blow and out would come these huge blood clots. The care team that he had assigned to him couldn't stop the bleeding.

He was given blood transfusions and platelets around the clock. They were trying everything they could do. Having treated Aaron as a patient before, the doctors were very familiar with his health chart. Although these seemed like dark times, we made the best of it. Our conversation got deeper and our love for each other had grown tremendously. From the very beginning we were not strangers to morbid conversations. Aaron looked at me as I cuddled under him and told me that he wasn't afraid to die, but he was afraid to leave me here with nothing. He wanted to ensure that if something happened to him that I would be financially secured. Not wanting to accept that death could be the outcome, I began to cry and this was the first time he's seen me cry about his health conditions since he was first diagnosed. Nothing else was said as he too began to cry. We accepted what could be and from that day forward all we wanted to do was to make the rest of our days together beautiful.

The agreement was to shed no more tears and just try to be in joy in each other's presence. His every wish was my command, and we did just that. He had been admitted into the hospital for a few weeks now. He spent the rest of January there. There was no improvement in his condition. Having exhausted their supplies, his care team made the conscious decision to have him transferred to another hospital. Because whatever was happening they knew it was beyond their knowledge and scope of expertise. If this happens at a hospital, usually this is never a good sign. In this moment I realized just how strong we both were. With mostly just him and I being the only consistent support system for one another we leaned on each other like never before. I could see the fear in his eyes just as he saw it in mine. Not knowing what was ahead of us, we vowed that no matter what, we would face it together. I left my car parked at Morristown Medical and rode in the ambulance with him this time. I held his hand all the way to the next hospital. Aaron was transferred to Hackensack University on Sunday February 2nd 2020 at 12:49am.

He hadn't seen much of our kids and was missing them dearly. Before Aaron was transferred from one hospital to the next I attempted to reach out to Cam's mother so he would at least get to see her for a short visit. She was being difficult at first and asking for pictures of everything from the family room to his room. Completely annoyed, I put my ego aside and obliged and she finally agreed for me to pick her up. But it was already too late-- Aaron was moved two days before our planned visit. Everything happened so fast and my hands were tied each day, between helping with my daughter's school schedule, and sleeping at the hospital again, but this time around we have a dog to care as well. I would go home after work, walk the dog, feed the dog, play with the dog all while doing homework with my daughter. There was so much happening at once that it all started to become a blur to me.

Being under so much stress I needed help. I found someone to at least help with the dog. He didn't live too far from us, which made it easy to check on Cleo and drop off her necessities. It really helped that he was a friend of the family who also had Cleo's mother and brother. Things were going well for a week or two until I received a phone call from him saying our dog had run off and was either lost, killed, or stolen. I was more upset for Aaron than I was for myself about this news. I packed my daughter up who had to be taken to her father after homework,and before I went to the hospital and went out looking for my dog.

I checked parks, drove down several streets calling her name. I had no luck. Finally getting my daughter to her father's house all I could think about was how I was going to break the news to Aaron. I made it to the hospital and Aaron's mother was there. They were having a conversation and when they were done talking there was an awkward silence. He looked at me and wondered why I was so quiet. So I just ripped the band off and told him that we no longer had a dog. At first he was okay then over the next five to ten minutes he was boiling over. I tried to keep his mind off of things by smiling at him. I was trying to find a silver lining in the situation. I said well at least that's more money we save on dog food and it's one less thing to worry about. So unsure if that came across as being insensitive or if it actually helped. He looked at me and said well maybe Cleo was unhappy there and tried to find her way home. I agreed and we moved onto another conversation.

There I was in a hospital waiting room. Staring at a clock on the wall, watching doctors walk past this little tiny window on the door. Some in panic, others with lunch, while some were discussing paperwork and patients' progress charts. I remember the feeling of fear and nervousness of not knowing which of these doctors were going to enter the waiting room and bear the news about my fiance. At that moment the pit of my stomach began to burn. As I am impatiently waiting, all kinds of thoughts are running through my mind. There wasn't any blood rushing to my feet. My feelings ranged from worry to hopefulness minute by minute. But nothing could have prepared me for what came next.

Holding my future mother in law's hand and waiting for the doctor to speak just made me more anxious. So I let go and allowed the doctor to say what she came in to say. She came in with questions and options, but her demeanor said it all, and the only thing I could think of while she was explaining it all was, *"oh my God he really isn't coming home this time"*. After the doctor presented us with the facts she exited the waiting room to give me and his mom a minute to process everything that was happening.

Cancer changes you-- it changes everything. The most difficult part of the caregiver role is keeping that person's mind positive. Keeping them in good spirits is an even harder task. As many times as I felt defeated at the surface, I knew that even though I struggled with bills, caring for our small family, work and the outside world. Still none of those things could compare to the harsh reality that he was facing with his second bout with cancer.

CHAPTER 8
JOURNEY TO WELLNESS

Aaron displayed such resilience throughout his entire battle with cancer, but this part of the fight was different. He had been hospitalized again and this time the leukemia was spreading rapidly. He could barely breathe without an oxygen mask. Not knowing what was happening day-to-day was the scariest feeling ever. Not knowing if death would be here to claim its next victim. Hearing beeping sounds from several machines around the clock while watching the love of my life dwindle away right before my eyes made it all too real.

This wasn't a dream or nightmare, it was all happening in reality. Aaron's health was deteriorating everyday and everyday the doctors were forming a plan. Tomorrow is never promised and we all knew that. Keeping that in mind his mom and I decided to call in family from both near and far. Within days his family from Ohio and a few members from New Jersey filled the hospital room. Aaron was so happy to see everyone. He hadn't seen his paternal grandmother or aunt and uncles in several years. You could immediately sense the love fill up the room as we all sat around and embraced Aaron during his toughest time.

Grandma Joann, his paternal grandmother and Sylvia, his maternal grandmother were both present. Amongst the loved ones were his 3 uncles Joey, Junior and Shylough, 2 aunts, Angie and Melissa and a host of cousins ranging from ages of 2 to 19. Both of his beautiful grandmother's played key roles in Aaron's life. He would spend summers with grandma Joann where he and his cousin Michael and the children she fostered would get into mischief. When school was in session he was in and around his grandmother Sylvia's. His family lived close when he was growing up in New Jersey before moving around state to state, so he had plenty of cousins to keep him entertained while his mother worked.

I hadn't seen Aaron this happy in weeks. Although he was weak and could barely move, that still didn't stop him from receiving all the love and warm hugs and kisses that surrounded him. This was just what he needed to begin his journey to wellness as his condition got worse over night. The next day the doctors were behind the scenes preparing to put their plan to save his life into action.

There was a nurse monitoring him closely while they waited for a bed to become available in the Intensive Care Unit (ICU). Silence filled the room as me, his mother, and his uncle Shylough waited patiently for him to be moved. The clock seemed to be moving so slow and the process had taken forever. After nearly half the day passed, finally it was time to transfer him to the ICU. By the time Aaron was prepared to be moved, a few more family members had come to visit. He had an entire entourage escorting him through the hospital as he lay in his hospital bed. Finally reaching the room, the doctors allowed us all time to give our well wishes because the next step was for him to be intubated. This is a procedure that is used when a patient cannot breathe on their own. The doctor puts a tube down the patient's throat and into their windpipe to make it easier to get air into and out of the lungs. The patient also has to be put to sleep during the process to allow easy access to the windpipe.

There was not one dry eye in the room except for mine and Aaron's. Everyone was preparing for the worst, but we knew for some reason that everything was going to be fine. In our heart of all hearts and the deep connection between us we just knew. After everyone was done giving him hugs and kisses, treating him as if they would never see him again, it was my turn, and everyone left the room to give us privacy. It was just me and my soulmate at last. He looked at me with so much love in his eyes and reassured me that he would be okay. I told him that I feel that he would be ok also. I dug into my pocket and asked for his hand. He opened his hand and I gently placed a totem in it. When he was first diagnosed, Aaron's mother had given him this small beautiful white guardian angel figurine that sat inside of thick glass that resembled a tiny snow globe. We had been looking for it around the house for a while, and as I was washing clothes one day, it fell out of his jeans pocket. I never told him that I found it until this day. As I handed it to him he couldn't help but to blush. I explained to him that it's his totem from the movie Inception, which is one of his favorite movies. Aaron is such a movie buff that he even turned me into one. I told him that when he's ready to wake up from the dream to just hold it tight. For those that aren't familiar with the movie Inception, each person in the movie has a small totem that would help them indicate whether or not they were awake or still in a dream. After giving him the totem I expressed how I truly felt at that moment. I was a little nervous, but I wasn't afraid because there was no way my Superman wasn't going to get through this.

We hugged each other tight and for a long time, I made him promise that no matter what he was coming back to me. We talked until the doctor asked me to leave the room. As I walked away I let him know that I would be right there when he woke up. We were all guided to the waiting area by a nurse. The room wasn't too far from the ICU. It was one big room with a whole bunch of chairs and a few vending machines and telephone charging stations. The room had the type of chairs that were very comfortable; some were even recliners. The vending machines had everything in them from coffee, fruit to junk food, which also indicated that people would spend a lot of time there while waiting to visit their loved ones. The nurse went on to explain how the visiting hours worked on this particular floor. There was a 2 hour window in between shift changes. This allowed the nurses to compare notes and give directives.

We all waited for the doctor to come and tell us how Aaron did during the intubation procedure. It was just as you see on TV--people waiting to either get good or bad news about their loved ones. The doctor came into the room and explained that he was going to hold off on the procedure because Aaron wasn't in as bad a shape as he seemed. What a relief that was. Everyone packed up to go home, feeling lighter about the good news we had received. A few family members stayed around to chat, but I stayed and waited to visit with my love before leaving the hospital. I stayed as long as I was allowed to. We sat and reflected on how far we've come together and how much of our journey was still remaining.

I cried a lot on my way home. I kept a brave face on for him in the hospital, but I felt as if I was dying on the inside. Filled with so many emotions, I could barely make it to the parking lot before the tears came falling down my cheeks. Everyday I came to the hospital with high hopes of Aaron's condition improving, but it seemed like everyday he had a different ventilator on his face. The machinery was only getting heavier. He was hooked up to a CPAP machine. The equipment had taken up his entire face and was really loud. Aaron was so upset and was beginning to get depressed because he wasn't able to talk much. We could only communicate by using sign language. Until one day his care team decided to no longer hold off on the intubation procedure. Aaron was struggling to breathe on his own. All those ventilators were no longer effective. I happened to visit with him when they made this decision. A team of doctors came rushing into the room and began using medical terms amongst each other that were foreign to me. One doctor asked who I was and I responded "I'm Aaron's fiance." I was then presented with a document that required a signature. This document was consent for him to undergo intubation. Aaron looked at me and agreed for me to sign.

My heart was pounding because it was happening fast. I sat and watched as they prepared him with an IV to administer the anesthesia. The nurse explained that he would be asleep for a day or so before they would slowly begin to wake him up using heavy sedation. They needed his body to rest so he could begin to heal. One doctor placed her hand on my shoulder and explained that they would do everything to make him better. I buried my face in my hands and bursted into tears. The nurses were in and out of the room grabbing equipment. It looked like traffic on a highway at the door. I watched as they put him to sleep and began putting the tube down his throat. It all happened in the matter of minutes. I stared as his limp body convulsed from the long plastic tube that entered his airway. I was in complete shock as I saw the love of my life move as if his soul had left his body. The doctor asked if there was someone they could call for me to be with while all of this was happening. It was a weekday and everyone was at work, so I was alone.

Aaron was under sedation for four days; two of which he was asleep and the other two, he was awake but heavily sedated. He seemed as if he were still not fully awake. I didn't miss a day; I would always stay until I was told that I had to leave by the nurses. I held his hand and sang to him everyday. His hands were so warm and his complexion on his face was beginning to return to its natural color. Not sure if he could hear me singing or could hear his mother's voice or even if he could hear Uncle Shylough's prayers. I wonder if he could hear when his father and uncle Alfie came to visit, but we did it anyway, and we never stopped talking to him and letting him know that we were all present.

By the fourth day I received a phone call from the hospital that woke me up from my sleep. I wasn't getting much sleep, but I jumped up in fear. I answered the phone and on the other end of the phone was a nurse. Her name was Barbara, and she went on to describe how Mr. Harvey had pulled out his own breathing tube, which sent all the nurses in a frenzy. Then she told me how he danced as he sat and waited for them to rush to his room in sheer panic. I laughed and cried so hard over the phone. She passed the phone to Aaron, but not before she told me how lucky I was to have him. I couldn't have agreed more. At first he forgot how to use his voice so he was whispering. I said "my peace, you can use your voice now baby." He took a second and then said "My Gravity, baby I love you so so so much." I felt the emotion behind every syllable of the statement hit me directly in my heart. He then said "tell my momma I love her. Eastwick, Exit 13, 'P.o.P' holdin' it down", and I couldn't contain my laughter.

When he was done talking, I let him know that his Superwoman was on the way to be by his side. He was so excited to hear me say that. I drove at least 80 mph down the New Jersey turnpike, risking it all in the name of love.

I arrived at the hospital in no time and I was so eager to wrap my arms around Aaron. Feeling him in my embrace was the only goal for the day. He was so happy to see me that he almost fell out of bed, as he forgot that he was still weak and wasn't able to leave the bed just yet. We were both very emotional as we reunited after his four day intubation procedure. Having never been apart for the past 2 years, it seemed like forever to us. He was getting better and looking great each day, but he still wasn't completely out of the woods just yet. He was moved back to a regular floor the day after and was already beginning physical therapy.

His doctor explained that in order to keep the leukemia from returning, Aaron would eventually have to have a bone marrow transplant, but there would be an alternative step before making that decision. The doctors wanted to try a new type of anti-cancer drug called Blincyto. It wasn't considered chemotherapy but it was referred to as a form of immunotherapy, but they were hoping it would help his immune system fight cancer. The great thing about it was that he was able to go home with it. Aaron just had to wait at least a week so they could monitor his reaction to the drug and help him to learn to walk again before he was released.

Sure enough a week later his reaction to the Blincyto went well and physical therapy helped tremendously. He was able to walk and was strong enough to go home! During our ride home we did what we always do--reflect. He couldn't remember much and I couldn't fill him in on the details without crying. So, he chose to wait until we got home to talk about it. When we reached home there was a ton of mail in our mailbox. I grabbed it and continued up the stairs to get Aaron as comfortable as possible. I helped him up the steps and onto a chair. I began opening some of the mail. It just so happens that the first envelope I opened was a court document. It appeared that while Aaron was fighting to stay alive again, his ex-wife was planning court dates for a custody hearing as if things weren't already complicated enough for us. So disgusted with her behavior, I just decided to not open any more mail.

Focusing on his health each day became second nature. I was cooking healthy meals and made sure he got out of bed and moved his body around. Within no time Aaron was back outside and back on his onewheel. This time he was riding around with a fanny pack full of Blincyto. Nothing could stop this man from living--not even immunotherapy.

We were in the beginning of the month of March and it was almost time for the custody hearing for his youngest daughter. I felt so bad watching him jump through so many hurdles just trying to stay alive, yet here he was having to fight his bitter ex to stay in his daughter's life shortly after. He eventually won shared custody so that was good news, but the roller coaster ride didn't stop there. After being granted more visitation for his youngest daughter, his oldest daughter was being forced to live with us by her mother. With no regard that Aaron's health was still recovering, her mother told Aaron that the reason for this circumstance was that she had no other choice but for her to come live with us, which I didn't think was not a reason at all. Here's where I had to really practice patience. It just seemed so unfair that he just couldn't catch a break from these bitter and clingy women. It seemed as if every chance they had, they would try to come in between Aaron and I by using his children at every cost.

Everything was being thrown at us all at once yet again. Although Aaron felt good most days, he still had some really bad days. In between some nights, he would be in so much pain that I would wake up to him crying and punching the wall, but that didn't seem to matter to anyone else. We had no help from anyone. Faced with the fact that we would now have a live-in child to care for on top of caring for Aaron's health, and still making time for my own child, while picking up his youngest daughter every Tuesday and every other weekend. Aaron has at least 2-3 doctor visits a week. I was at the end of my rope; my only escape for my own sanity was going to the grocery store and taking walks. If I didn't then I was going to explode. It was never that his daughter wasn't welcomed to stay, it was just the inconsiderate behavior that her mother often displayed. She has a few other children and had a new live-in boyfriend, so he was more important to her than her own children. Under these circumstances it was way more than I thought I could handle.

I would always question, *What if he didn't have me? Would she have still done this to him?* Trying not to become upset just made me even more upset about the situation. So I just let it be and made peace with it, because if I didn't, then my thoughts would consume me and I would become just as bitter as they were. Aaron and I talked and communicated frequently. He was really concerned about how I felt about it all. I told him exactly how I felt about it. This was a very uncomfortable conversation because I never wanted to say the wrong thing and upset him or even worse, have him think that I didn't want his daughter to stay with us. We talked and I came to the realization that she was better off with us anyway. Having been the oldest of four children Grace wasn't being cared for or heard as much as she should have been.

Grace was settling in well and we were all doing our best to adjust. Our relationship as future step-mother and step-daughter began to blossom. Grace would be so shy and I just made her feel as comfortable around me as possible. It was different from us just picking her up on the weekends and her returning to her mother. Now she was with us full-time and had already lived with a step-mother who wasn't nice to her, so she was a little leery about it, and I understood that. We were big on communication in our house, so I spent a lot of one-on-one time with her until she felt like she could tell me anything. Things were beginning to look up--so we thought.

We approached the middle of March in what became the global pandemic of COVID 19 as if things couldn't have gotten any worse. We were just getting a rhythm and routine of going between doctor visits and finding a babysitter on those designated days. We were creating a balance in our lives and our daughter's as well, and now this. We had been following the number of cases when Aaron was in the hospital, but at one time, there weren't many reports of cases in the United States. That reporting changed rapidly. One of the first cases was reported right at Hackensack University, where we were just located a few short weeks prior. As the death toll began to rise, we found ourselves in a quarantine lockdown situation. No one was allowed to go anywhere except to grocery stores.

Aaron wasn't allowed to go too many places anyway due to his health, so it didn't bother him at all. I was home at the time already. I had taken a leave of absence from work to care for him. Grace wasn't in school at the time either because we had to transfer her from Pennsylvania to the New Jersey school system. With no help from Grace's mother, things were difficult trying to get the proper credentials that were needed.

We didn't know what was going to happen next. All I knew was that Aaron had to be kept safe because he had a compromised immune system. So after my trips to the store I would come inside and strip off all my clothing and wash my hands thoroughly before I even came near him. No one knew what was to be expected. Everything came to a stand still, I mean the entire world stood still with the rise of the COVID pandemic. People worried about future plans of weddings that were already paid for, businesses were losing money, and landlords were still asking for rent. We, on the other hand, were worried about how Aaron was going to get his bone marrow transplant that he was scheduled for in July. The government had no answers as to how long we would be in quarantine. So we just went with the flow of things. We still went to doctors appointments at the cancer center. The doctor still had plans to stick to schedule.

When July came things were slowly trying to get back to normal. Everyone still had to wear masks and more stores were opening for at least half the day. Night life was a thing of the past and finding tissue was such a scarcity. Nonetheless, we were still on schedule. Aaron went in for his transplant after seeing a series of doctors. This time I couldn't be by his side to hold his hand and sing to him as I have been doing the entire time he was sick. Because of the pandemic no one was allowed into the hospital if they weren't a patient. We had no clue how we could stand to be apart for an entire month. Besides, even if there was no pandemic we now had a child at home that couldn't take care of herself. Everything happens for a reason right?

We ended up going back to the basics of when our relationship first began. We would choose beautiful places all over the world to meet in our dreams. We would send screen shots and take turns choosing destinations. Before bed he would Facetime me and I would tell him to meet me at *Harvey'z World* sometimes.

Aaron's presence and energy was always felt; he would tell me how he could feel my energy and love surrounding him as well. After ALL of that was said and done, what helped us survive was remembering and constantly reminding each other of where it began, and why we set out on this journey together in the first place. No one said it would be easy, but love, communication, trust, respect and understanding held us together.

"I love you with everything I am, everything I've been, and everything I hope to be. I love you with my past, and I love you for my future, and for the years we'll have together. I love you for every one of my smiles and even more, for every one of yours."

Julia Quinn

CHAPTER 9
THE FINAL CHAPTER

Summer time is supposed to be filled with fun and full of laughter. Pool parties, barbeques, and outdoor fun with the ones we love is what summer meant to me. This summer looked very different for us all though. Although the lockdown didn't carry out throughout the summer, everyone was still being cautious and staying 6 feet apart. The playground was the only solution to our boredom. Aaron was in the hospital until the end of August, but seemed like an eternity. So most of summer it was just me Grace and Sky. Grace didn't like the outdoors too much. I think it had something to do with her being in her pre-teenage years. We've all been there, thinking we were going to find ourselves by locking ourselves away and hating the world. She was also becoming homesick and missing her father. So I'd constantly beg her to come out with me to get some fresh air, hoping it would make her feel better. I think it helped a little. Aaron and I spoke all day everyday when he wasn't out in the hallway for his daily walk or next door at his neighbor's room trying to convince him to walk with him, or catching up on his sleep. He asked about the girls all the time.

I would update him on Grace's mental health--experiencing being bounced from one house to the next, then a pandemic--all while her father is in the hospital again. Grace has experienced so much, not to mention being stuck with her future stepmother whom she still wasn't 100 percent comfortable being around. She was dealing with a lot for a 12-year old.

I told him that she definitely missed him. He knew exactly what to do. The next day I had to swap out his dirty clothes for clean ones. I also put together a care package with all of his favorite snacks, since we were still in the middle of a pandemic. The hospital still wasn't allowing visitors unless there were special circumstances and patients weren't allowed to come to the lobby. So I would have to call the nurses station on his floor when I arrived at the lobby. A nurse would come down and escort the items that I had brought for him. This was my fourth or fifth trip in one month, and I made Grace come along for the ride this time. Usually she would be asleep until the late afternoon, but I woke her up and I'm so glad that I did.

Aaron always had a way of being *"the magic man"* for our girls--kind of like every dad's quarter trick. "What's in this hand and what's in this hand?" You think the trick is over, but he's always got something else up his sleeve. The girls would always be in awe. We arrived in the lobby and I was on the phone with Aaron the entire trip there. He was informing me that someone was coming down to retrieve the package. We waited for a while--longer than usual. He asked me where exactly we were standing. As I looked around to give a landmark all I saw was him being pushed towards us by a nurse. In complete shock, Grace and I ran to hug him. Still being mindful of outside germs, our visit was brief. All three of us had tears in our eyes, and we even had the nurse in tears. It was just what we all needed. I have no clue how he pulled it off, but we were so happy to see him! Even for a brief moment.

Aaron came home that following week and we all were elated. We had never spent that much time apart before. He called that morning and was told he would be released. I ended up taking that ride alone. Grace opted to stay with her great grandmother. As I pulled up in front of the hospital it felt like the first day

I visited his place. I looked in every mirror and was so nervous. I was so anxious I began to shake my leg and twirl my thumbs. It seems that it had taken them forever because he had a lot of stuff to pack up. Finally the moment of truth came. I saw the man of my dreams being pushed toward me in a wheelchair wearing his green Jets cap, khaki shorts and white Adidas sneakers and a huge smile. We met in the middle of the lobby and greeted each other with the most endearing hug--just like the first hug we shared. Everything stopped, and it seemed as if every object stood still! There were no people walking in the waiting area, no voices were heard and it was as if time stood still for an entire 60 seconds. We put all of our broken pieces back together with a single hug. When we finally let go you could hear about 10 or more people say "awwww."

Summer was nearly over and again Aaron found himself having to adjust to home life. A few weeks prior I had to empty out the entire apartment by myself. There was an inspection and I had to make it appear that no one lived in the attic. What a task that was. As frustrating as it was, it had to be done. The silver lining was that I had the opportunity to give the apartment a deep cleaning and change a few things around before Aaron's arrival. He appreciated everything I had done just for his comfort and safety.

Fall proceeded forward and Aaron still had to be cared for as if he were still in the hospital. He still had a triple lumen catheter inserted into his chest. This is a central line that was placed for the purposes of blood sampling and administration of medication since he had to be poked and prodded on a regular basis. The line prevented his veins from deteriorating. Aaron came home, and a nurse had come to the house that day and gave me a training course on how to take care of the catheter. I was given very clear and simple instructions, but I was so afraid that I would do something wrong. So Aaron walked me through it until I was comfortable. I also received a call from a nutritionist two days prior to receiving the training. I was given specific instructions on how to prepare his food and what he was allowed and couldn't eat. My head was spinning from taking in all this new information in just a few days while still recovering from packing and unpacking our apartment by myself. Realizing that his life was truly in my hands to the fact that if I cross-contaminate any food he could possibly die. If I didn't clean the catheter properly, he could contract an infection and die. The pressure was on.

I was exhausted and overwhelmed, but left with no choice. I had to slap the superwoman "S" on my chest as I always do. We were under the impression that there would be a nurse that would come every week to help and check on things. But I think after she climbed our steps, she had changed her mind. Also we were in the middle of a pandemic, and her job was already dangerous enough. So we did what we had to do and didn't complain. We would receive packages every week from the hospital. They would send supplies that were needed to clean his central line and saline. I had to hang a four hour bag of hydration to his IV after having to administer immunotherapy. I wore many hats at once. I played the role of a mother/stepmother, fiance', therapist, and now a nurse. Not to mention, I was picking my mother up from work everyday while Aaron still had to attend three doctor visits per week. Rest was nowhere in my vocabulary. Thankfully by the third week, the catheter was removed, and I was relieved of my nursing duties.

By October, Aaron was doing well at home and becoming more active. His hair was beginning to grow back--it began to fall out during radiation. His legs were stronger so he was on the onewheel even around the house. We were able to pick up Cam for visits again, and he wasn't confined to the bed anymore. Some nights would be challenging; Aaron had to digest twenty-six pills in one day. His gut and digestive system was not adjusting well to this regimen so he would literally be awake crying and punching the walls throughout the night. Sometimes he would cry silently so he wouldn't wake me. I always sensed his cries and would wake up anyway. I would hold him while we tried to find a solution to the problem. We tried everything: Tums, Pepto Bismol, laxatives, steroids. We found that Alka Seltzer was the best solution and thank God for aspirin! I never liked questioning: *What else could go wrong?* Because in our world something else would always go wrong.

One day as I was driving my mother home from work the craziest thing happened. I left the house fifteen minutes early to pick her up from work as I always did. Aaron was preparing to take a ride on his onewheel to clear his mind. I had my daughter with me because her and Grace were not getting along for whatever reason. So I took her with me to give them some space as Grace stayed indoors to play video games. On the way home, my mother, Sky and I were talking and laughing when a car ran through a stop sign at an intersection and hit us! We were hit in the rear driver side of my car, which then caused us to spin into a utility pole. As the dust from the airbags filled the car, I went into shock and paused for a few seconds. I could smell the scent of what smelled like ammonia. When I snapped out of it, I could hear my daughter crying for help from the backseat while still strapped in her seatbelt. My mom was struggling to breathe and holding her chest. I didn't know what to do at first so I tried not to panic and calmed myself. I sprung into action trying to free my daughter from her seatbelt. I looked in on my mom and she was ok. A few bystanders had helped her onto the sidewalk. After ensuring that we were all safe with minor scrapes and bruises, I called Aaron and let him know what had happened. He showed up in a few short minutes. Skylar's father showed up moments later along with the ambulance and a firetruck. We went to the hospital at about 3 o'clock and we were home by dinner after a series of tests were taken to assure we didn't break anything or have any serious injuries. I was just grateful that we made it home at all. We were thankful to have escaped with a few scrapes, aches, pains and anxiety.

Life as we knew it continued on. Cam had a soccer game that following weekend so we loaded up our rental car and made our way to see her. Still at odds with her mother, Aaron made sure he made it to every game just to be sure he was as present as possible in her life. He wanted her to know his love for her meant the world to him even though her mother tried to paint the picture in a completely different way. During the soccer game Aaron's mother showed up with her dog and his younger brother. We hadn't seen her since she moved to Florida a month or so earlier. We were happy to see them--all the kids were especially excited to be in the same space.

Shortly after their arrival, we were presented with a few questions by his mother. It was apparent she was in a bit of a situation. She had just moved out of state not too long ago so it was a little strange that she was back so soon. We figured maybe she had to tie up some loose ends. Then she asked if we could take in her and his younger brother for a few days. Without hesitation, we agreed to let them stay with us. We still had a lot going on and were very limited on space, but we didn't mind helping her.

One day into their stay, she had become ill and Aaron was still struggling with his own health issues. I thought I was going to lose my mind; I had a full house and only two hands. Eventually his mother had recovered and took a flight back to Florida, but she left his brother behind with us. A few days ended up becoming a few weeks. I was so worn out and tired at this point. His brother was not a problem at all--he is the sweetest kid. The problem was that we were all inconvenienced at the wrong time. Dare I mention we had no space for the amount of time he stayed. The girls were complaining about having a boy in their room all the time which left them with no privacy. There was constant noise between video games being played in both rooms and our two youngest children running through the house. My humble home was turned upside down.

As if our lives weren't complicated enough we now took on more issues that were not even our issues to deal with. This began to cause a rift in our relationship; too much was happening because I was already wearing many hats and taking on too many roles. To top this off, someone else's problems were thrown on top of ours. It just seemed like there was no consideration for our schedule which was already hectic. I felt like it was expected of me to be this strong resilient woman who couldn't be broken, and I was supposed to shut up and just deal with it. Well I was nearing my breaking point. Aaron and I would get our wires crossed over the smallest things; I would snap at the drop of a hat. We never operated this way and it was unusual for me to be so bothered by little things. He saw the toll it was taking on me and had a serious talk with his mother. He explained that it's not that we didn't want to help her, but we simply couldn't help any longer.

She understood, and our house eventually returned to normal. Thanksgiving was just around the corner, and we had planned a trip to Ohio to Grandma Joann's house. Aaron wanted to drive and I was still struggling with anxiety in cars since the accident, so he left the decision to me. I wanted nothing to do with sitting in a car for six long hours. I know he wanted to go because we haven't seen them since they came to see him in the hospital. I slept on it for a few days and finally the day came to give an answer. We woke up with smiles on our faces as we usually did. I said, "let's go!" Still waking from his slumber, he said with such excitement, "Yeah?! You sure babe?! The last thing I want is for you to be uncomfortable." I responded, "yes I'm sure love--we need it." Aaron jumped up and grabbed the suitcase and started packing our clothes, and yelling in the next room for Grace to get dressed. I watched from the bed, laughing as he scrambled from one end of the room to the other. That was by far the best decision I had made that day. We picked up Sky on the way, and set off on our journey.

We arrived by nightfall and what an amazing trip it was. As soon as we walked in the door we could smell freshly baked cookies in the air. Besides cookies, we were greeted with so much love; we received a hug around every corner. We could literally feel the love as soon as our feet stepped into this house. We had a wonderful time--Aaron was in his glory. He rode his Uncle Joey's motorcycle every day we were there. He helped with the setup to fry the turkey for Thanksgiving.The girls and I played on the trampoline and found other ways to entertain ourselves. Grace got a new haircut and I was so happy that I got a chance to meet everyone on this side of Aaron's family. On the way home he held my hand as he drove down the long twisty roads. He said to me ,"babe I'm so glad you decided to take this trip. I'm glad you got to see what made me different." I couldn't have been more honored that he shared that with me. That trip was just the reset that our little family needed. Even though Cam wasn't allowed to come with us, she was there in spirit.

When we arrived home it was back to the same rat race, but our spirits felt much lighter. Aaron and Sky's relationship had improved and so did mine and Grace's. We felt so much closer as a unit. We listened to each other better and more attentively. Instead of yelling when the girls did something wrong we would talk it out. Instead of getting agitated, we would give each other hugs. Our household looked a lot different.

We still had issues with Cam's mother and were spiteful by trying her best to interrupt Aaron's weekends with her, especially around the holiday season. For the past two years when Christmas was approaching there was always an issue with visitation. There was always a reason or excuse as to why our time with Cam would have to be interrupted, and then Aaron would alway end up in the hospital. So he would have to wait weeks until he saw his baby girl again. This holiday season we were hoping it would be different, but unfortunately it wasn't.

We were on our way to pick up Cam for our two hour Tuesday visit. We were literally two seconds away from her house when Aaron received a text message from her mother stating that she may have the Covid-19 virus. Aaron had read the message to me and I immediately asked if he still wanted to pick Cammie up. With concern that she too could have contracted the virus from her mother, but much like every holiday season, we figured this was another lie or excuse as to why he couldn't see his daughter. We were already outside of her house when she sent the text and he was missing his daughter like crazy so we proceeded with the visit. Just to be on the safe side as a precaution, we all kept our masks on during the visit.

During every visit before we dropped Cam off back with her mother, she would ask why they couldn't have more time together. It was such a heart wrenching question because Aaron had been fighting her mother for her in and out of court for months all while he had a fanny pack full of immunotherapy pumping through his body. Aaron attended court date after court date during the custody battle. There were days where he would have chemo the day before and felt terrible, but that never stopped him from fighting for his daughter. While this was all happening Cam's mother's boyfriend would attempt to intimidate Aaron by trying to pick a fight. He thought he was a tough guy because he was a part of a gang. Aaron wasn't afraid; he was just too sick to fight if it ever came down to punches being thrown.

It broke my heart to watch her try to break the man that I love, but I also knew that the situation had nothing to do with me. I would always let it be known that no matter what, I had his back; I was never too far. As we dropped Cam off she had revealed that she was still sleeping in the same bed as her mother while she was experiencing Covid -19 symptoms. Aaron had explained to her why it wasn't a good idea for her to be sleeping with her mother. He told her she could possibly get sick as well. She's a child so he explained the best way he could to make her understand. A few days later Aaron was beginning to feel regular cold symptoms: sniffles, headache, and puffy eyes, which was still a concern because he had a compromised immune system. When he told me how he was feeling I was almost positive it was just a simple cold, but we both were thinking that he may have contracted Covid-19, yet we didn't want to say it out loud. Especially since he was already experiencing bad anxiety. He had an upcoming doctor appointment on December 8th at the cancer center so we waited and took necessary precautions around the house.

Aaron went to the doctor and it was protocol for him to be tested for Covid every week. This visit he had to tell the nurse about his new symptoms. He also explained how he visited Cam that prior Tuesday. He even gave her a little bit of the background story on his ex-wife. He shared how he thought she was lying about having the virus just to make up an excuse for him not to see his daughter. After being swabbed for Covid testing, the nurse came in bearing bad news. She said "well, Mr. Harvey, your ex-wife wasn't lying this year. You tested positive."

When Aaron arrived home and told me the news, I could see the concern in his face. I on the other hand was ready for whatever obstacle came our way. We had already been through so much regarding his health that I was ready to face this virus head on. He was so nervous about passing it onto us; whereas all I wanted to do was to cuddle up under him. He wore his mask around the house and tried to wear it to sleep. I debated with him about sleeping with it on. He said, "Well, it's either I sleep with it on, or I move to another room." At that point I didn't care about catching any virus, I just wanted him to be ok and comfortable. So I compromised by wearing my mask instead of him not being able to breathe all day.

Grace stayed in her room most of the day anyway and so did we. There wasn't much space to work with in our apartment, but we made it work. As I mentioned before, Aaron struggled with anxiety, and he tended to over monitor himself constantly. I had to literally take away the oximeter and any other instruments that he used to monitor himself with. I put on a movie to try and take his mind off of the situation, but that didn't last long at all.

Aaron was so worried and trying to get him to relax was becoming an ordeal. He finally decided that his oxygen level was low and he wanted to call his doctor. I tried keeping him as calm as possible because the last thing I wanted was for him to have a full on panic attack. So I made the suggestion of taking a xanax first just to see if it was just his anxiety getting the best of him. He took the xanax and after a little bit of time had passed he still wasn't satisfied, and was almost at the point of hyperventilation. I made him look me in my eyes as I always did to keep him calm followed by some kind and encouraging words. We called his care team that night and before I knew it, we were instructed to go to the Emergency Room. This was three days after finding out that he had tested positive for Covid.

As we approached Hackensack, we noticed there was a McDonald's at the corner before reaching the hospital. We went through the drive-thru to order food. By this time, Aaron was calm. Maybe driving helped keep his mind off of things. Aaron, Grace and I shared a meal in the car. We talked about a few things on the way. He actually thought I was mad at him for whatever reason. I had explained that he hadn't done anything wrong and we hugged and kissed as usual. I said "ok babe, how are you feeling?" He said "funny thing , I feel ok, I'm breathing ok." I turned and replied, "yay!" So we ate dinner in Hackensack. "Let's go back home," even though I said it as a joke, something inside me was screaming for him not to go into the ER that night. But I knew his mind wouldn't let him rest, and given his track record we agreed that we wanted to be safe rather than sorry. We reached the entrance of the ER and he hugged Grace and told her to behave for me. Then he turned to me and told me how much he loved me while he kissed my forehead. He then grabbed my face and looked me in my eyes and said "I'll see you soon my 'Gravity'." I said while holding back tears "hey my 'Peace', just make sure you come back to me ok." He pinky promised me that he would. We hugged each other a little longer and a little tighter that night, which was odd because he hated long goodbyes.

Peace and gravity, these two forces were at the center of our world. Peace is a concept of societal friendship and harmony in the absence of hostility and violence. Aaron always leaves an impact wherever he goes--it never mattered who or what. He just knows that he could spread peace and positivity through his inspiring words and his kindness toward others, he did just that. No one ever wanted him to leave the room because his light shined so bright.

Gravity is gravitation, a natural phenomenon by which all things with mass or energy including planets, stars, galaxies, and even light are brought towards one another. Aaron would always explain why he called me *"Gravity"*. At first it was just because I held him down by always being there with him. I called him *"Peace"* because that was always the way he made me feel--at peace, but as our love grew. It became more about the way I cared for him and others around us, and the fact that I simply just understood him. I also had respect for the way he designed his life. He became a beacon of light for so many people. This is what kept him fighting through all of his sickness and health, and it also kept me strong enough to help him fight through those dark days. I was the glue that kept us all together, while Aaron led us to the light. I would often tell Aaron that none of this works without him. He would respond "No, babe it all works because of you."

When Aaron contracted the Covid-19 virus there was no doubt in our minds that he was going to beat it. Just as he did cancer, twice before. We just knew that love was going to carry us through just one more time. This time it wasn't the case. Since the doctor had called us to come to the hospital in the middle of a pandemic, it was already a bad sign.

After waiting in the waiting room for hours and not being able to see or touch Aaron for weeks,the only thing I wanted to do was rush to his side and hold his hand. The doctor walked us into his hospital room and I felt a burst of energy behind me. As I held his cold hand I knew that his spirit was no longer with his body. As crazy as it sounds I felt his energy behind me, not in front of me, where his body laid. At that moment I couldn't breathe so I pulled off all the safety gear and walked out of the room. It's really hard to explain why I couldn't cry in that room. I guess I didn't want him to feel that I was in pain. I didn't want him to feel how off my energy was by seeing him this way. I felt like I had to be stronger than I ever had to be for him. Walking back to the waiting area and leaving his mother there for her personal time with him, I wondered if a miracle could happen. Aaron was always pulling rabbits out of his hat. *"This can't be it,* I thought, feeling confident that he would wake up. Shortly after the doctor walked in behind his mother and I already knew there was no good news. Both of them sat down and began to explain what the options were. His mom made sure they explained exactly what was about to happen. Somewhere in my mind I knew before it was even said out loud. She uttered the words but my brain still couldn't process what was happening. Her words moved in slow motion as she said "he's not getting any better and your only options are to take him off of life support and we'll give him meds so he doesn't feel any pain, or we take him off of life support and allow his heart to pump until it stops."

There I was faced with the hardest decision I ever had to make in my life. It just wasn't fair that either way the love of my life was going to die. I felt my heart sink into my feet. My fingers had no feelings in them and went numb. I thought I was going to faint. Still I couldn't cry, as I uttered the words, "I just want to die", and for a moment the room fell silent. Still tears wouldn't come out; I was too hurt to cry. I gasped for air and tried to process it all. I took a deep breath and gathered myself and his mom and I agreed to have the breathing tube removed to allow the doctors to administer medication to make him comfortable. It had taken some time for them to start the process, because we asked them to hold off until his best friend, who is more like his brother, arrived. He finally made it and they had us all put the safety gear back on. They kept us close to the door because it was going to happen quickly. So we sat by the door until they called us into the room and his mom and brother on his right side, and me on his left side. We held his hands as we watched him take his final three breaths. He gasped, just as I did in the waiting room while being told that I was physically losing the love of my life. My soulmate, the one person in the world that understood me and

I understood him back. It's almost as if I was already prepared; like a foreshadow. The energy that I had felt earlier while standing next to his hospital bed had already let me know what was expected to come. Just as Aaron would always prepare me for anything coming our way in life.

PEACE & GRAVITY

I am writing this book because I believe that the love story that my fiance Aaron and I have lived is inspiring in so many ways. If we survived what should have destroyed us before his death. Then you too can make it through anything. Somehow and in some way sharing our story will enlighten someone in their quest or journey to stay connected to loved ones whether in life or in death. Believe me, it was not a walk in the park; we were tested every step of the way during our relationship. It's a love story that made it through the craziest of circumstances. But, we only got stronger together. It's a story of how we overcame obstacles by being spiritual and staying true to one another by using simple life tools! We had survived the rest of his life together by using the essentials which are love, trust, communication, understanding, patience, loyalty and respect. We tested the limits of love and survived through persistence.

My very first sentence of this book was a question: *Ever wondered how the universe works?* After Aaron's death I sat in and around nature quite often. I would sit and wonder if he was with me while I sat and cried as I fed the ducks. Or if he was wiping my tears as I listened to a song I wrote especially for him as I sat under the cherry blossom tree? Or what part of the universe he had transitioned to? Or if he had wings and how beautiful I know they are if he does. I came to the conclusion that nature is where I would find these answers. The universe speaks to us through nature, it's all around us. We are forever evolving, take for example the beautiful butterfly. Let's explore how a butterfly's life is developed through a process of metamorphosis. Which means transformation or change in shape. At first it's an egg, then a caterpillar, transitions to the pupa (chrysalis), and lastly becoming a butterfly--one of the most beautiful creatures on earth. How does this compare to life?

We all begin life as our mother's egg first. Then we become this little tiny seed, and we cocoon for nine months before you know it a beautiful little human is born. Aaron believed that our children are proof that we are ever evolving. Through learning life's little lessons as toddlers to when they become teenagers and begin to form their own opinions about life. We all have to change because we never stop learning; we never stop growing. Who you were, who you are, and who you will be are three different people.

I truly believe that Aaron is never far. I still very much feel the embrace of his love and energy all around me. Energy or love cannot die; he just outgrew his body and had to evolve. He served so much purpose in this lifetime and touched the lives of so many. His legacy will continue to live on through us all.

I found myself dancing with the ocean and couldn't help but imagine you dancing with me as we once did. As I stood at the edge of the murky water I went back to that very moment in September under that Florida sun. I closed my eyes as I felt your presence, I felt your soft touch as you wrapped your arms around my waist. I imagined the kiss you laid upon the back of my neck and I heard your voice as you explained how you couldn't find the words to explain how deeply and truly you loved me. I pictured your smile as I expressed gratitude to God for blessing me with you.

I know that physically you are no longer here. I can't just reach for a hug because I feel like you're not close enough, even though you're sitting right next to me. But I will continue to hold on to every moment that we shared just as I did this one.

Someone asked me: What made him so special? My response was and will always be: He was everything that I am.

ACKNOWLEDGMENTS

This book is here because of the love, support and effort of so many people. There are so many to name but here's a start:

Josephine Sanders: My amazing and gorgeous mother , my everything, and number one supporter. You are the first person I call for everything. Without you, I would not be here to experience all that life has to offer. Your heart of gold and beautiful personality has been the most perfect example for me to refer to when I felt like giving up. You are the epitome of a strong woman. I love you and I am blessed and lucky to be your daughter.

George Harrell: Daddy thank you for treating me like a princess and giving me unconditional love that every little girl deserves. I know wherever you are, Aaron is there with you and the scenery is beautiful.

Dana L.Harvey: My beautiful mother-in-law. With your kind heart, fun, loving personality, and the love of a mother is what shaped and molded the man of my dreams. Without you there's no way I would be telling this story. I love you and thank you for sharing this wonderful soul with me. You are the queen that birthed my king. I am forever grateful.

Joann Delprete and Sylvia Harvey: Where do I begin with these two wonderful women-- Joann: the moment we met I knew we would get along fine. The embrace of your hugs are long lasting and unforgettable. Sylvia, as soon as you saw me you knew exactly who raised me. From my great grandmother (Eldora Sanders), my grandmother (Margret Carol) down to my parents and made me feel right at home in the Harvey family. Without these women helping and wrapping their arms around Aaron as a child he wouldn't have been the man we all know and loved. God put a little something special in grandma's hands.

Sherrie Elle: Your patience, kindness, dedication, and ability to create help bring this book into existence. You are truly a guiding light in this world and I am so grateful to you!

Horacio and Michele Palaez: Thank you so much for your endless support! There were days that I didn't wanna get out of bed or answer the phone. None of that stopped you from calling or coming by. I can't begin to thank you enough for dropping everything and always making sure that me and the girls were okay. Love you guys!

Michael Carter: Your witty conversations, conspiracy theories, and sense of humor kept Aaron going plenty of days. You two were like two peas in a pod. Listening to you both speak with such intelligence on a regular day was really something to see. I'm really glad that he had you as his cousin/brother. Thank you for having those conversations that I wasn't able to have with him and thank you for accepting me as the third pea.

Gio and Vanessa: Thank you guys for being a part of my support system. From the very beginning your kind words and visits got me through some tough days. Making sure I was eating was a challenging task at one point but you were up for the task. G, thank you for being a part of the wolfpack! Forever grateful for you guys!

Brother Russia: Good friends are hard to come by but lifetime friends who become family are rare. Aaron would tell anyone in a heartbeat that you are his brother, not just a friend. I'm so happy that I too get to call you my brother.

Corey and Ailin Sanders: Life throws us in so many directions at the most unexpected times and sometimes it's just hard to keep track of our siblings and their families. But we never fall off track even with the many miles between us we still manage to remain intact. Thank you for accepting Aaron the moment he walked through the door. He loved the fact that he instantly became "uncle A-A ron." I love you!

Danny, Lisa, Wesley, and Malissie: Growing up in the same house made us so close. All the petty fights and clothes stealing somehow only made us closer. Thank you for all those experiences that helped shape me. I love you guys always.

Josh and Letishia: "Our homies!" Meeting you guys in the hospital during such a trying time was all by design. It was so comforting to know that we weren't alone in the struggle. To actually have genuine people in our corner while we were all learning how to balance it all each day made it just a little easier to deal with the circumstances. We are still and will always be grateful for the gift of you.

Special thank you to the generations of the Avery and Harvey families before us that kept our families intact throughout the years!

This book is dedicated to the life and loving memory of Aaron F. Harvey.

This book is dedicated to the life and loving memory of Aaron F. Harvey and our beautiful daughters Grace Harvey, Cambria Harvey, and Skylar Williams, you three will always and have always been our driving force and the reason that daddy fought so hard to be here.

My love, our time here on earth was short but we had already lived an eternity together. I love you unconditionally and I will choose you in a billion lifetimes, infinite worlds, and every version of reality I will always choose you. I will continue to walk on our journey until we meet again my peace.

"To laugh often and much; to win the respect of intelligent people and the affection of children; to earn the appreciation of honest critics and endure the betrayal of false friends; to appreciate beauty; to find the best in others; to leave the world a bit better whether by a healthy child, a garden patch, or a redeemed social condition; to know even one life has breathed easier because you lived. This is to have succeeded."

RALPH WALDO EMERSON

ABOUT THE AUTHOR

DOMONIQUE HARVEY is a self-published author who aspires to become a speaker and life coach to help others cope with the loss of a loved one. She is currently living in New Jersey, in that third floor attic apartment with her daughter and her dog. Dominique will soon relocate to the state of Florida.

Instagram: @DomoniqueHarvey

Made in the USA
Middletown, DE
06 November 2024